70000042077

KT-514-300

£12.99

718

WITHDRAWN
FROM STOCK

express
housekeeping

7000042077

express housekeeping

How to speed clean Lighten the laundry load Tidying tricks & tips

Anna Shepard

WITHDRAWN FROM STOCK

Editor Hilary Mandleberg
Art Editor Miranda Harvey
Photographer Howard Shooter
Illustrator Sean Sims @ New Division

DK UK
Senior Editor Scarlett O'Hara
Senior Art Editor Jane Ewart
Editorial Assistant Kajal Mistry
Managing Editor Dawn Henderson
Managing Art Editor Marianne Markham
Senior Jacket Creative Nicola Powling
Senior Presentations Creative
Caroline de Souza
Senior Production Editor Jennifer Murray
Senior Production Controller Alice Sykes
Creative Technical Support Sonia Charbonnier

First published in Great Britain in 2011
by Dorling Kindersley Limited,
80 Strand, London WC2R 0RL

Penguin Group (UK)
2 4 6 8 10 9 7 5 3 1
001 – 179888 – Mar/2011
Copyright © 2011 Dorling Kindersley Limited
All rights reserved.

No part of this publication may be reproduced,
stored in a retrieval system, or transmitted in any
form or by any means, electronic, mechanical,
photocopying, recording or otherwise, without
prior permission of the copyright owner.

A CIP catalogue record for this book
is available from the British Library.
ISBN 978-1-4053-6307-5

Printed and bound in Singapore by
Tien Wah Press

Discover more at **www.dk.com**

Contents

WITHDRAWN FROM STOCK

Introduction

At last! Now there's no need to spend half your life cleaning your home. With the expert tips, tricks, and time-saving strategies in this book, you can get it all done with maximum speed and efficiency – most of the tasks in the following pages take less than 10 minutes to do (excluding soaking, standing, and drying times).

Cleaning little and often is the smart, pain-free way to keep the dust and dirt under control – that plus regular decluttering. There's no greater time-waster than sorting and tidying before you even reach for the vacuum cleaner, so keep your house in order and you're halfway to keeping it clean.

And you don't need a huge stock of cleaning equipment and chemical cleaners. Your everyday kitchen store cupboard contains items that clean just as well as branded products – and they offer an appealingly greener and thriftier alternative.

If you're juggling a full, busy life with running a home, this book is a life-saver. You'll get the house sparkling clean, super-fast – so you can get on with the rest of your life!

Basic kit

It's impossible to create one cleaning kit that suits every scenario, but here are the basics. Invest in a plastic tote to carry your kit around the house with you as you work. You're more likely to keep the dirt under control if you can grab the product you need quickly. The key to keeping your home clean with minimum effort is to tackle jobs promptly and do little and often.

BLEACH
Use to disinfect and prevent mould and mildew.

DISINFECTANT SPRAY
Use for bathrooms or kitchen counters.

PLASTIC TOTE
Useful for carrying your cleaning kit round the house with you as you work.

DUSTERS
Use these for buffing up a surface after polishing. The eco alternative is a piece of old t-shirt.

MICROFIBRE CLOTHS
Use these dry or slightly damp for almost any job where you need a cloth.

SCOURERS
Use for scrubbing pans. Buy plastic ones for non-stick pans.

CREAM CLEANER
Good for quickly
removing marks from
many surfaces.

FLOOR CLEANER
Choose a type that suits
your flooring.

SPRAY BOTTLES
Use for applying
eco-friendly home-made
cleaning solutions.

RUBBER GLOVES
Wear for most cleaning
jobs to protect your hands.

PLASTIC JUG
Useful for mixing small
amounts of cleaning
solutions.

Store-cupboard kit

You'll probably need a bigger store cupboard for larger items. Here are the essentials to help you get your home cleaned to perfection. Keep the things you use most often, such as the dustpan and brush and the vacuum cleaner, near the front of the cupboard for quick access.

VACUUM CLEANER
Probably the most useful appliance in your cleaning tool kit. Choose one with at least 2 or 3 attachments.

BROOM
Use for quick sweeps instead of getting out the vacuum cleaner.

LONG-HANDLED DUSTING BRUSH

Use to dislodge cobwebs and dust from hard-to-reach places. Unlike feather dusters that spread the dust, these nylon filaments pick it up.

PLASTIC BUCKET

A bucket with a mop wringer quickly and efficiently wrings out the traditional type of mop pictured below.

FLOOR MOP

Use a modern version with strips made from a mixture of microfibre and cotton for washing hard floors. These mops are lightweight and dry quickly.

DUSTPAN AND BRUSH

Use for small spills and mess. This neat design keeps the pan and brush together in the cupboard, making them easy to find in a hurry.

Natural cleaning kit

It's hard to believe that some of the best household cleaners are natural ingredients, but once you've tried vinegar on windows or bicarbonate of soda on stained mugs, you'll quickly realise their value. Many of these items may already be in your kitchen cupboard. If not, you'll find everything you need in a supermarket, chemist, or hardware store. Make sure you equip yourself with a few spray bottles, too, for applying your home-made cleaning solutions.

SOFT CLOTHS
Use soft knitted cloths made from natural cotton to buff items to a shine.

BICARBONATE OF SODA
A gentle alternative to using abrasive cleaning products.

BORAX
Good for bleaching whites and deodorizing.

VINEGAR SOLUTION
Made from water and white vinegar, spray wherever you want to break down limescale.

LEMON JUICE
The acid in lemon juice helps dissolve limescale and, combined with salt, it can remove stains.

TEA TREE OIL
A natural disinfectant, it works particularly well on mould and mildew.

Speed Cleaning

10 MIN Emergency tidy up

If your house is in chaos and you have limited time before visitors arrive, don't worry. It's amazing how much you can get done in just 10 minutes – especially once you're armed with our useful checklist of tasks.

1 BE SELECTIVE
Don't try to tidy the whole house. Just think about the main area(s) you want to look clean. They're likely to be the kitchen and living room, and you'll probably want to include a whizz around the bathroom. ✓

2 DISPOSE OF RUBBISH
To eliminate bad smells, make sure you dispose of full bags of rubbish. Then open the windows to let fresh air in and perhaps light a few fragranced candles. ✓

3 CLEAR THE TABLES
When tables are de-crumbed and clean, everything will look much better. If there's any paperwork lying around and adding to the clutter, pile it into a box file or folder. ✓

4 CLEAR THE KITCHEN SINK
This might involve doing a bit of light washing up, putting away any dry dishes, and/or loading the dishwasher. ✓

5 TIDY THE LIVING ROOM

Clear the coffee table and put books and magazines away. Then pile everything else that's cluttering the living room into a basket and tuck it in a corner or another room to sort out later.

6 DEAL WITH CHAIRS AND SOFAS

Check chairs and sofas for crumbs, then plump the cushions and neatly fold any throws over the arms or backs of chairs and sofas.

7 STRAIGHTEN THE RUGS

You won't have time to shake out rugs, but just straightening them and picking up any crumbs and other debris makes all the difference.

8 WHIZZ ROUND THE BATHROOM

Don't get caught up in proper cleaning here. Just wipe around the sink and behind the taps, check the toilet's clean, and tidy cosmetics.

9 BLITZ THE HALL

Hang up coats and items of clothing. Pile shoes, hats, and other clutter into a hallway basket – keep one in the hall for this purpose.

10 HIDE THE REST

Hide rooms you haven't tidied by shutting the doors, then adjust the lighting in the rest of the house so dirty corners can't be seen.

Dust surfaces

Dust little but often to keep household dust at bay. Most modern surfaces are designed for easy cleaning – all they require is a quick damp-dust. Dry-dusting takes a little longer, but you need only dry-dust non-washable wall surfaces and furniture made from solid wood. Always vacuum after dusting to collect the dust that's settled.

→1

Dust the walls and ceiling, including the corners. Use an extendable brush with nylon filaments. These pick up the dust instead of spreading it around like a feather duster.

→2

Use a damp microfibre cloth to dust any washable surfaces. Be sure to collect the dust by folding it into the cloth and getting rid of it, rather than simply moving it about.

WHAT TO DO WHEN

DAILY → To keep on top of your dusting, get into the habit of dusting something every day, even if it's just a table.

WEEKLY → Dust coffee tables, lampshades (see box opposite), and electronic equipment (use an anti-static cloth for this).

MONTHLY → Dust walls and ceilings, skirting boards, and bookshelves.

Quick dust for a lampshade

First unplug the lamp, and leave the bulb to cool. Holding the lampshade steady, dust it gently using the dusting-brush attachment and your vacuum cleaner. Work the brush into any gathers or creases. Avoid bending the shade out of shape. Gently dry-dust the bulb then wipe the base.

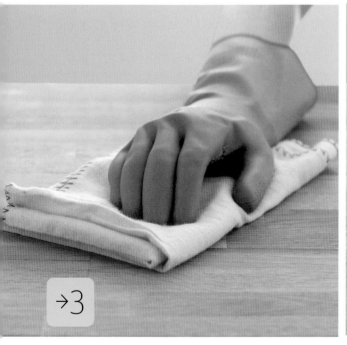

→3

Use a clean duster or a dry microfibre cloth to dry-dust non-washable surfaces. As you work, use oval motions. You are aiming to gather the dust beneath the duster.

→4

Fold the duster to trap the dust, then repeat step 3 with the folded duster. When the duster is too small to continue, shake it out carefully into a bin, and start again.

Vacuum kit

Investing in a good vacuum cleaner is a major step forward in the battle for a clean home. The main choice is between an upright model, which is good if you have large areas of floor to clean, and a cylinder model, which is best if you have to cope with a lot of stairs. Choose a vacuum with a variety of attachments, then you'll be able to tackle a surprising number of jobs around the home very speedily. Many vacuum cleaners incorporate on-board storage for the smaller attachments.

UPHOLSTERY NOZZLE
Use to vacuum sofas, cushions, curtains, mattresses, and similar furnishings.

CREVICE NOZZLE
Vital for getting into corners and crevices.

DUSTING BRUSH
Useful for dusting hard surfaces.

ALL-PURPOSE FLOORHEAD
Vacuum carpets by retracting the brushes and hard floors by extending them.

TELESCOPIC TUBE
Adjust the length of the tube so you can vacuum without stooping.

VACUUM CLEANER
If you opt for a cylinder model, make sure you can comfortably carry it around the house.

HOSE
Today's vacuums have non-kink hoses so the suction power isn't impeded. Choose a model that allows you to adjust the suction – gentler for rugs and curtains, and more powerful for floors.

FILTER
If you have allergies or pets, choose a vacuum with a High-Efficency Particulate Air (HEPA) filter that traps the finest particles.

DUSTBAG
Dustbags are easy to empty but you need to keep a supply of spares.

5 MIN Vacuum a carpeted floor

Vacuum your carpets frequently to help lengthen their life. With today's efficient vacuum cleaners, the job only takes a few minutes and there's no need to move the furniture every time.

BARE ESSENTIALS

vacuum cleaner

carpet floorhead

crevice nozzle

Before you vacuum, pick up any stray bits of paper, food, or other debris from the carpet that might get sucked into your vacuum cleaner and block it.

Either use the carpet floorhead or adjust your upright cleaner for use on carpets. Starting at the far side of the room, vacuum back and forth, using repeated, overlapping strokes.

WHAT TO DO WHEN

EVERY FEW DAYS → Vacuum areas of carpet that get a lot of use. Ground-in dirt will shorten the life of the carpet.

EVERY FEW WEEKS → Pull out beds, tables, and chairs, and vacuum the carpet beneath.

EVERY 2–3 YEARS → Have your carpets professionally cleaned. If there are children or pets in the house, do this every year.

Extra tips

There's no need to set the vacuum cleaner to maximum suction when you're cleaning a fitted carpet. This will make the job harder and will weaken the fibres of the carpet. Instead, set the vacuum to medium suction and don't press down too hard – let the vacuum cleaner do the work.

→3

→4

Work towards the door, still making repeated, overlapping strokes. Go over dirty patches several times as the cleaner will pick up more dust each time.

When you have finished vacuuming the main area of the carpet, attach a crevice nozzle and use this to clean along the skirting boards and in the corners.

5 MIN Vacuum carpeted stairs

You don't have to vacuum stairs more than once a week. The key to doing it speedily lies in the preparation. Clear debris and clutter before you begin, then the job will only take a few minutes.

BARE ESSENTIALS

vacuum cleaner

crevice nozzle

carpet floorhead

→1

Start by collecting any debris on the stairs that is big enough to clog your vacuum cleaner. Look out for things like coins, paper clips, and bits of paper.

→2

Attach the crevice nozzle to the vacuum cleaner and use it to clean thoroughly in all the corners, where the treads meet the risers, and along the skirting boards.

Extra tips

Stairs are often used as dumping grounds for things that are either on their way up or down. For speed and safety as you work, remove any clutter before you begin.

To save time, plug the vacuum cleaner in at a socket that's located conveniently so that you can vacuum as many stairs as possible before you have to unplug it and plug it in again somewhere else.

If you are using a cylinder cleaner, you will have to perch it on a stair and move it as you go. Starting from the bottom and working upwards means there's no risk of the machine falling on you as you work.

Using the carpet floorhead or adjusting your upright cleaner for use on carpets, start vacuuming on the bottom step. Vacuum the tread – the horizontal part of the stair.

Swivel the floorhead so you can run it along the riser – the vertical part of the stair. Repeat on each stair, continuing until you reach the top.

Maintain a vacuum cleaner

Modern vacuum cleaners are quick and easy to maintain and should give years of useful service. It's worth spending a few minutes changing the dustbag and checking the filter regularly to keep it working efficiently.

BARE ESSENTIALS

clean vacuum bag

clean vacuum filter

microfibre cloth

bamboo cane

→1

Change the dustbag when it's full.
Always do this job outside or in a well-ventilated area following the manufacturer's instructions.

→2

Check the filter regularly and replace when necessary following the manufacturer's instructions. Make sure that it stays free of debris so it works efficiently.

Extra tips

Although they don't have a bag, today's bagless vacuums need emptying too. Empty the dirt container when it's three-quarters full, and occasionally rinse it out and leave it to dry. You also need to clean the filter. It's recommended that you do this every time you empty the dirt container. Follow the manufacturer's instructions.

Look after the exterior of your vacuum cleaner too. From time to time, unplug it and give the wheels a quick wipe with a damp cloth. This removes dirt, which marks carpets, and grit, which damages wooden floors. If you use the vacuum outside to clean the interior of your car, stand it on a rubber mat to stop the wheels from picking up dirt and grit.

→3

Check the floorhead once a month.
Remove any bits of string or hair that have collected on the brush, then give it a wipe with a damp microfibre cloth.

→4

If your vacuum stops sucking efficiently, the hose may be blocked. To remove the blockage, gently push a bamboo cane down. Don't use force or you risk causing damage.

10 MIN Clean curtains

Cleaning curtains is easily overlooked but doing it will help prolong their life. It's a quick and easy job and you only need to do it once a year. In between, simply vacuum them from time to time.

BARE ESSENTIALS

vacuum cleaner

dusting-brush attachment

washing line

sponge

handwash laundry detergent

→1

Close the curtains then vacuum them, moving from top to bottom along the entire width of the curtain. Use the dusting-brush attachment and minimum suction.

→2

Turn the curtain back to vacuum the wrong side. Again, vacuum from top to bottom. Take care to clean this side thoroughly as it often gathers most dirt.

Cleaning Roman blinds

A Roman blind made from a fabric that is washable can be laundered, but it will involve unstitching the blind and sewing it back together afterwards. A speedier alternative is to use a foam upholstery cleaning product. Try it out first on an inconspicuous area of the blind to make sure that the colour in the fabric doesn't run. After you've applied the cleaner, wipe it off carefully using a dry cloth. If upholstery cleaner doesn't work, you'll have to call in a specialist cleaner.

Prevention is better than cure, so vacuum Roman blinds regularly with the dusting-brush attachment. You can also have the blind treated with a stain-resistant finish.

→3

Take the curtains down and shake them well outdoors to remove any dust you may have missed. Hang over the washing line to air – preferably outside – for several hours.

→4

With the curtains on the line, check for stains. Remove them, using a barely damp sponge and a little handwash laundry detergent. When the curtains are dry, re-hang.

10 TIPS Rug and carpet care

The shoes-off rule is the answer to many people's effort to keep carpets clean. Others prefer to make fewer demands of guests and put up with the consequences. Either way, you'll need to vacuum rugs and carpets regularly and check for stains.

1 USE GOOD UNDERLAY

When laying new carpet, choose good-quality underlay for extra cushioning. It also helps prevent dirt from being ground into the carpet and makes it easier to be collected by the vacuum.

2 FLATTEN CURLING EDGES

If the edge of a carpet or rug starts to roll up, press it flat or someone might trip. Lay a damp pressing cloth (a square of linen or cotton cloth will do) on the edge and iron it firmly using a medium setting.

3 USE A DOORMAT

Use doormats at each entrance to your home, ideally inside and outside. This makes a big difference in preventing rugs and carpet from gathering dirt.

4 KEEP THE CURTAINS DRAWN

If light is making a favourite rug or carpet fade, try to keep the curtains drawn at sunny times, especially if the room isn't in use.

5 LIFT THE FURNITURE
Always lift furniture when you move it around a room. Never push or drag it across the carpet as this will damage the pile.

6 RE-POSITION RUGS
Turn rugs around regularly or change their position to even out wear and avoid damage done by furniture. It will also help to even out fading caused by sunlight (see tip 4).

7 BEAT OUT THE DUST
A couple of times a year, ideally on a bright, windy day, take rugs outside, fling them over the washing line, and beat them with a broom or tennis racquet. Seek professional advice for a valuable rug.

8 VACUUM REGULARLY
This is your first line of defence. Vacuum rugs and carpets every week. Dirt and dust make rugs and carpets look grubby, and they hasten the appearance of worn patches.

9 AVOID WASHING RUGS
Unless otherwise advised by the care label, the general rule is that it's best to avoid washing rugs. Instead deal with individual stains with warm water and carpet detergent.

10 AVOID OVER-CLEANING
Professional carpet cleaning ages carpets so try to avoid getting them dirty in the first place. As long as you vacuum regularly, you can get away with professional cleaning only once every 3 years.

10 MIN Clean a venetian blind

Blinds look fiddly to clean but they needn't take long. And you don't need specialist equipment – just a vacuum cleaner and a damp cloth. Do this quick clean with the blind still hanging at the window.

BARE ESSENTIALS

vacuum cleaner with dusting-brush attachment

microfibre cloth

all-purpose cleaning spray

→1

→2

Lower the blind fully and close the slats. Keeping the blind steady, gently dust the closed slats using the dusting-brush attachment on your vacuum cleaner.

Now open the slats of the blind and vacuum them again. This time, make sure that you get the brush into as many nooks and crannies as possible.

Quick cleans for other blinds

Vacuum vertical blinds using the dusting-brush attachment or a special blind-cleaning tool.

Clean non-washable roller blinds by vacuuming with the dusting-brush attachment. From time to time, take the blind down, lay it on a clean flat surface, and vacuum the back.

Clean washable roller blinds with a well-wrung-out sponge and upholstery shampoo. Rinse each side by sponging with clean water, and drying with an old towel. Re-hang it while it's still a little damp.

Vacuum wooden venetian blinds with the dusting-brush attachment or use a dry sock worn on your hand. Avoid using water.

→3

→4

With the slats still open, wipe the blinds with a damp microfibre cloth or with a dampened sock worn on your hand. Make sure you don't bend the slats as you work.

Close the slats and if there are still any marks, squirt them with an all-purpose cleaning spray. Finish by wiping with a damp microfibre cloth.

10 MIN Quick window clean

When you haven't got time for a full-on window clean, you can easily get away with a quick wipe and polish. Just focus on the dirty bits, leaving a thorough clean to be done once or twice a year.

BARE ESSENTIALS

measuring jug

spray bottle

white vinegar

sponge

microfibre cloth

→1 **Make a mixture of** 1 part white vinegar to 4 parts water and use this to fill a plastic spray bottle. This home-made window-cleaner works as well as bought products.

→2 **Before you spray the window,** wet a sponge, squeeze it out and use it to remove the worst of the fingerprints, smudges, and other dirty marks on the glass.

ACTION PLAN

BEFORE YOU START → Move furniture out of the way for easy access to the window.

AS YOU WORK → Spray the vinegar and water mixture sparingly or it will involve more work to buff and dry.

AFTERWARDS → Rinse the vinegar from your sponge before you put it away.

Quick mirror clean

Quickly buff a mirror to a shine using a microfibre cloth squeezed out in water. If the mirror's very grubby, squeeze a sponge out in warm water mixed with a little washing-up liquid. Wipe the mirror with the damp sponge, then buff it with a dry microfibre cloth.

→3

→4

With a clean, squeezed-out sponge at the ready, spray the vinegar solution on the window, one area at a time. Use the sponge to rub the solution in.

Still concentrating on one area of the window at a time and working quickly to avoid streaking, buff the glass dry using a dry microfibre cloth.

25 MIN Thorough window clean

Once or twice a year, clean your windows thoroughly, including the frames, to remove any dust and mildew. It won't take long, and windows and frames will stay clean for several months.

BARE ESSENTIALS

microfibre cloths

washing-up bowl

bleach, knitted cloth

bucket

white vinegar, sponge

→1

Start by dusting the frame with a dry microfibre cloth to remove any cobwebs. Make sure you dust every surface of the frame, both vertical and horizontal.

→2

Wipe the frame with a soft damp cloth, then, to eliminate mildew, make a solution of 1 part bleach with 3 parts water. Wring the cloth out in this, then wipe again.

BEFORE YOU BEGIN

ARRANGE A TOWEL → Lay a towel on the sill or on the floor, to collect any water drips.

MOVE FURNITURE → Get all furniture out of the way so you have safe and easy access to the windows.

SET UP A STEP LADDER → Essential for high windows. Make sure it's securely erected.

Extra tips

Stubborn marks on windows can be removed with undiluted methylated spirits. Apply it directly to the mark on one cloth, then rinse with a clean cloth squeezed out in water.

Polish and dry in step 4 using scrunched-up newspaper. This old-fashioned technique works on mirrors too.

→3

Make a 1:4 solution of white vinegar and water in a bucket. Squeeze a sponge out in it, then drag the sponge over the window from the top down. Rinse and repeat.

→4

Working quickly to avoid streaking, polish the window with a dry microfibre cloth. Work as before, starting at the top and moving down.

15 MIN Kitchen speed-clean

Cleaning your kitchen from top to bottom is a task that could take you all day. But follow this speedy routine and you'll get all the important jobs done in just a matter of minutes – especially if you stay focused on the task in hand.

1 **DEAL WITH DIRTY DISHES**
Scrape unwanted food into the compost bin or normal bin, then wash up or load the dishwasher. If you're washing up, leave the dishes to dry while you tackle the other jobs.

2 **TACKLE DIRTY PANS**
Put away any clean saucepans and frying pans. Fill heavily soiled pans with hot water (use cold for remains of proteins, such as egg) and a squirt of washing-up liquid, and leave to soak.

3 **WIPE THE HOB**
Wipe with a damp sponge and use a squirt of all-purpose cleaning spray to remove any stubborn stains. ✓

4 **AVOID GETTING DISTRACTED**
Try not to get distracted by reorganizing cupboards and drawers, instead simply focus on putting things back where they came from.

5 STORE FOOD AWAY

Store leftover food in suitable containers in the fridge. When you put food packages away in cupboards, check that they're securely closed.

6 GATHER UP STRAY ITEMS

Using a basket, collect items that belong in other parts of the house and recruit a helper to put them back.

7 WIPE COUNTERS AND TABLES

There's no need to get involved in proper cleaning. Just wipe surfaces with a damp cloth and all-purpose cleaner, to gather up crumbs and wipe away any marks.

8 DISPOSE OF RUBBISH

To reduce unpleasant smells, get rid of the rubbish and line the bin with a new bag. Put any wine bottles, newspapers, and other recyclable items in the recycling bin.

9 SWEEP THE FLOOR

Whizz round the kitchen floor with a broom to gather up a pile of dirt, then collect it with the dustpan and brush and throw it away.

10 VACUUM THE FLOOR

If you've still got time once you've got rid of most of the crumbs and dust by sweeping, quickly vacuum the floor using the hard-floor attachment.

5 MIN Clean the kitchen counter

Bacteria gather on kitchen counters so keep them clean to avoid picking up a bug. At least once a week, follow this speedy cleaning drill. There's no need to use an anti-bacterial spray – hot water and detergent will do the job.

BARE ESSENTIALS

washing-up liquid

sponge

waste bin

all-purpose cleaning spray

microfibre cloth

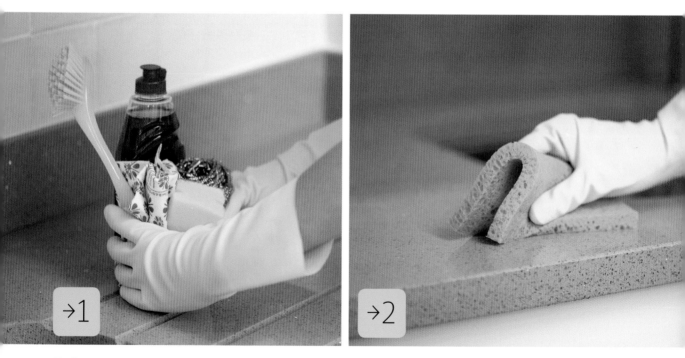

→1

→2

Before you start, clear the counter so the whole area is ready for wiping. Then fill a sink with hot water and add a squirt of washing-up liquid.

Gather any crumbs from the counter using a sponge squeezed out in the soapy water, shake the crumbs into the waste bin, then rinse the sponge in clean water.

WHAT TO DO WHEN

DAILY → Wipe up crumbs and spills as you go to avoid a build-up of mess.

WEEKLY → Follow the steps below. Also wash all your kitchen cloths and sponges in hot soapy water and scrub the draining rack.

MONTHLY → Unplug countertop appliances and wipe them clean with a damp cloth.

Extra tips

To clean dirt from grouting on a tiled counter, use a 1:4 solution of bleach applied with an old toothbrush.

Despite their durable appearance, granite and slate surfaces can scratch, so don't use an abrasive pan scourer to clean them.

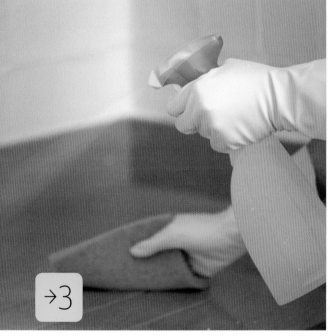

→3

Spray the counter with an all-purpose cleaning product, then wipe with the damp sponge, trying to remove as much cleaning-product residue as possible.

→4

Polish the counter using a clean, dry microfibre cloth. As well as leaving the counter shiny, this will remove any last traces of cleaning product.

5 MIN Clean the kitchen floor

Kitchen floors get a lot of use and get dirty quickly, however they usually only need a thorough clean once a week. This fast mop-and-bucket technique will give you a spotless, germ-free floor in minutes.

BARE ESSENTIALS

vacuum cleaner

floorhead for hard floors

bucket with a mop-wringer

floor-cleaning solution

floor mop

→1

→2

Before you start to wash, get rid of surface dirt and crumbs by vacuuming the floor with the vacuum adjusted for hard floors, or by sweeping.

Half-fill a bucket with warm water and add the recommended amount of floor-cleaning solution. Choose the correct type of solution for your floor.

ACTION PLAN

BEFORE YOU START → Clear any furniture out of the way to speed things up as you clean.

AS YOU WORK → Start at the far side of the kitchen and work towards the door. That way, you won't have to step on the wet floor.

AFTERWARDS → Don't walk on the floor until it's completely dry or you'll grind dirt back in.

Extra tips

Use the technique shown here on laminate flooring, but be sure you wring the mop out really thoroughly to avoid damaging the finish. The mop should be almost dry.

If you have a stone floor, seal it regularly, following the supplier's instructions, or water will stain it.

→3

Dip the mop in the bucket and wring it out thoroughly. Mop the floor using elongated oval strokes. Repeat until you have mopped the whole floor.

→4

If your floor-cleaning product requires rinsing, refill the bucket with clean cold water. Use the technique in step 3 to remove all traces of soap. Leave to dry.

Oven kit

Whether you've got a gas or electric oven, a fan or conventional one, the best way to keep it clean is to give it a wipe with a damp cloth after every use. The same is true of microwave ovens. But there are always times when tougher measures are called for and that's when you need some kit. Here is everything you need. If your oven's self-cleaning, your job's simpler – you only have to wipe away the ash residue.

KITCHEN TOWEL
Useful for applying bicarbonate-of-soda paste to a dirty oven.

SCOURER
Use to remove burnt-on food from pan supports and from burners.

MIXING BOWL
Use when you are making your bicarbonate-of-soda paste.

BICARBONATE OF SODA
Mildly alkaline, this cuts through greasy residues without the need for harmful chemicals. Mix it into a paste by adding a little water. Don't use on self-cleaning panels.

CREAM CLEANER
Useful for cleaning the exterior of the oven as well as electric plates with greasy residues.

OVEN CLEANER
A branded oven cleaner is useful for blitzing dirt from a neglected oven.

ALUMINIUM FOIL
Use to line the bottom of your oven to save on cleaning time.

LAUNDRY DETERGENT
Good for soaking oven shelves before you clean them.

DOUBLE-SIDED SPONGES
Wipe away crumbs with the sponge side; scrub burnt areas with the abrasive side.

RUBBER GLOVES
Remember to wear these when using any oven-cleaning product.

10 TIPS

Oven cleaning

If you've neglected your oven for ages and don't have the self-cleaning kind, you may need a chemical cleaning product to shift the grime. Follow the manufacturer's instructions carefully. These products can be hazardous.

1 READ THE INSTRUCTIONS
Many chemical cleaning products contain caustic soda, which can burn the skin, irritate the eyes, and harm the lungs. Keep the windows open and be sure to follow the directions on the product.

2 WEAR RUBBER GLOVES
Wear rubber gloves for all stages, from applying the chemical cleaner to wiping it off. When you've finished, rinse the outside of the gloves with hot water.

3 TAKE CHILDREN OUT
Consider going out when you leave the oven cleaner to do its work. This is especially important if you have young children, as it lessens the chance that they'll come into contact with the product.

4 PROTECT THE FLOOR
Before applying the oven cleaner, spread newspaper on the floor under the oven to collect drips: the cleaning product may damage the floor.

5 KEEP THE ROOM VENTILATED
Make sure you ventilate the kitchen well while you're cleaning the oven. Open windows – and doors, if possible, too.

✓

6 PROTECT YOUR SKIN
Wear long-sleeved clothing and avoid splashing the product on your skin. If you do, wash immediately with soap and plenty of water.

✓

7 PROTECT YOUR EYES
Chemical cleaners can irritate the eyes, so some manufacturers advise that you wear eye protection. If you get any in your eyes, rinse with plenty of water and see a doctor if they're still irritated.

✓

8 CLEAN OVEN SHELVES
Most products can be applied to oven shelves as well as oven surfaces. If shelves are particularly blackened, you may have to scrub them with a scourer before you wipe away the cleaning product.

✓

9 USE DISPOSABLE CLOTHS
Wipe off the cleaning product with paper towels or with cloths that you can dispose of afterwards.

✓

10 REMOVE PRODUCT COMPLETELY
After you've removed most of the cleaning product, swap to a cloth rinsed in warm water. Use this to wipe the oven repeatedly until you're satisfied the product's all gone.

15 MIN Clean the oven

To clean a filthy oven, you have little choice but to turn to a branded oven-cleaning product. If the oven isn't too dirty, try this non-toxic alternative. Use it regularly, then you won't have to turn to chemicals.

BARE ESSENTIALS

non-scratch sponge

small mixing bowl

bicarbonate of soda

kitchen towel

washing-up bowl

→1

Using the soft side of a non-scratch sponge squeezed in soapy water, gather up any crumbs from the interior of the oven. Rinse the sponge and wipe again.

→2

Make a paste by adding a little water to some bicarbonate of soda in a bowl. Using some kitchen towel, coat the interior with the paste, then leave to stand, ideally overnight.

BEFORE YOU BEGIN

TURN OFF AN ELECTRIC OVEN AT THE MAINS → Water and electricity don't mix!

MAKE SURE THE OVEN IS COOL → If the oven's hot, wait until you can safely put your bare hands inside.

REMOVE THE SHELVES → This gives you more room to manoeuvre. For how to clean the shelves, see pp.50–51.

Using a chemical cleaner

When all else fails, use a branded oven-cleaning product (see pp.46–7). These are highly toxic, so read the instructions carefully. Be sure to protect your skin from splashes, open the window, and lay newspaper on the floor to catch any drips. Leave the product on for the recommended time, then rinse thoroughly.

→3

→4

Squeeze the non-scratch sponge out in clean warm water and use the abrasive side on the oven interior to scrub off any stubborn burnt-on patches of food.

Wring out a clean sponge in a bowl filled with warm water, then use to rinse away the scum and dirt. Rinse and wipe repeatedly until the oven is clean.

5 MIN Clean an oven shelf

To clean off food that's stuck to an oven shelf, the principle's the same as when cleaning a burnt pan (see pp.112–13). Deal with the shelf as quickly as possible and start by soaking it in laundry detergent.

BARE ESSENTIALS

laundry detergent

metal scourer

→1

→2

Fill the sink with hot water. Add a capful of laundry detergent and submerge one shelf at a time. You will probably have to lay it diagonally.

If you can only fit half the shelf in the sink, after 15 minutes, turn it round to submerge the other half. Leave for another 15 minutes.

WHAT TO DO WHEN

DAILY → When the oven is cool, remove what burnt food you can from the shelves with your fingers.

WEEKLY → When the oven is warm, give the shelves a quick wipe with a damp cloth to remove the worst of the grease and debris.

MONTHLY → Remove shelves from the oven and clean them following steps 1–4 below.

Extra tip

If your oven shelves are suffering from neglect, take them outside, spray with an oven-cleaning product, then put them inside a bin bag. Leave for a couple of hours then rinse, preferably at an outdoor tap. Finish by washing in warm soapy water in the sink.

→3

→4

Use a metal scourer to scrub burnt-on food from the bars of the half of the shelf that was soaked first. Turn the shelf around and repeat on the other half.

Empty the sink and wash away the blackened debris from both sides of the shelf under running water. Leave the shelf to dry before replacing in the oven.

15 MIN Clean a fridge

To help keep your fridge clean and keep smells at bay, wipe up any food spills as soon as they occur. Then you'll only need to give the interior a thorough clean every couple of months. Wipe the exterior weekly.

BARE ESSENTIALS

washing-up liquid, sponges

measuring jug

bicarbonate of soda

spray bottle

washing-up bowl

→1

Remove the shelves and drawers from the fridge and place them in a sink filled with warm water and a squirt of washing-up liquid. Wipe them clean with a soapy sponge.

→2

Make a solution of 2 tsp bicarbonate of soda and 1 litre (1¾ pints) warm water in a spray bottle. Use with a sponge to remove stains from the interior of the fridge.

BEFORE YOU BEGIN

TURN OFF AT THE MAINS → Water and electricity are a dangerous combination.

EMPTY THE FOOD FROM THE FRIDGE → Keep in a cool place or cool box while you work.

VACUUM BEHIND→ Pull the fridge out and use the vacuum with its dusting brush on the coils and fan. Clean around the filter too, if your fridge is an ice-making model.

Extra tips

To keep the fridge fresh when you've cleaned it, sprinkle a teaspoon of bicarbonate of soda onto half a lemon and place it inside the fridge. Replace every couple of weeks.

Don't use a scourer to clean the outside of the fridge. Stick to a soft sponge and an all-purpose cleaning spray.

→3

Fill a washing-up bowl with warm water mixed with a squirt of washing-up liquid. Apply the soapy water on a sponge to wipe clean the interior of the fridge.

→4

Dry the shelves and drawers then replace them in the fridge. Finish by moving the fridge back into position, plugging it in and replacing the food.

5 MIN Descale and clean a kettle

If your kettle's coated with limescale it won't boil efficiently. It can also affect the taste of hot drinks. This eco-friendly descaling method works fast, whether for a stove-top or an electric kettle.

BARE ESSENTIALS

measuring jug

white vinegar

lemon

microfibre cloth

washing-up liquid

Make up a solution of equal parts white vinegar and water in a measuring jug. Fill the kettle with this solution, ensuring it's not so full that it bubbles over when it boils.

Bring the kettle to the boil and leave to soak overnight or for a minimum of two hours. After soaking, pour the vinegar solution away.

WHAT TO DO WHEN

DAILY → Empty the kettle each evening so you always start with fresh water next day.

WEEKLY → Give the outside of the kettle a wipe to remove streaks and stains every time you clean the kitchen counter.

MONTHLY → Follow the steps below to keep your kettle limescale-free.

Quick clean with descaler

Branded descalers are less "green" and can irritate skin and eyes, so use with care. Half-fill the kettle with water, bring to the boil, unplug (if electric), and stand in the sink. Gradually add the descaler. Leave for at least 30 minutes, then empty, rinse well with cold water, refill, boil, and empty again.

Rinse the kettle thoroughly, refill with fresh water and boil again. Pour this water away. If there's a vinegary smell, fill it with fresh water again, boil, and pour away.

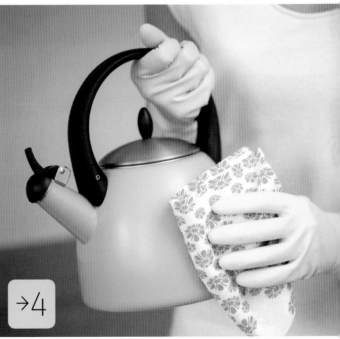

Rub any marks on the outside with the flesh of a lemon, then wipe with a microfibre cloth squeezed out in warm soapy water. Rinse then dry with a dry cloth.

55

3 MIN Clean a stained mug

Coffee is a natural dye and tea contains tannins that stain, so it's not surprising you get unsightly marks on your mugs and cups. Fortunately, there's a speedy eco-friendly solution to getting rid of stains.

BARE ESSENTIALS

bicarbonate of soda

old toothbrush

non-scratch sponge

washing-up liquid

→1

Sprinkle a little bicarbonate of soda in the mug then add enough boiling water to cover the stains. Leave to stand for at least 30 minutes.

→2

Pour the solution away and, using an old toothbrush, scrub the stains with the bicarbonate of soda residue. Make sure you reach right down to the bottom.

WHAT TO DO WHEN

DAILY → Don't leave coffee or tea dregs in mugs. Wash as soon as possible after use with hot soapy water.

WEEKLY → Use a washing-up brush to scrub any mugs that are starting to get stained.

MONTHLY → Identify any stained mugs and clean them following steps 1–4 below.

Extra tips

Fill the mug with a solution of equal parts boiling water and white vinegar. Leave overnight, then scrub with a non-stick sponge, wash, and rinse.

For the toughest stains, pour a teaspoon of bleach into each mug, then fill with boiling water. Let the mugs soak for 5 minutes, then rinse well.

→3

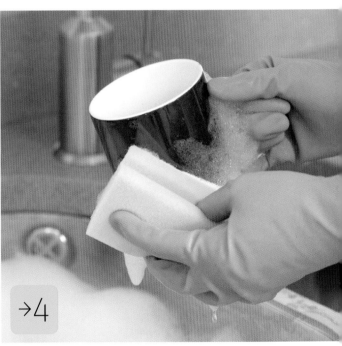

→4

If there are still any stains remaining that the toothbrush hasn't shifted, rub them gently using the abrasive side of a non-scratch sponge.

Once you're sure all the stains have gone, finish by washing the mug with your usual washing-up liquid and warm water. Rinse, dry, and put away ready for use.

Recycling kit

Much of the rubbish you create in the kitchen can be recycled or composted. This will save your dustbin from filling up too fast. If you compost, it will also help keep the dustbin clean as you won't be putting food waste in it. Store your recycling containers in an easy-to-reach place so recycling doesn't feel like extra work. If you don't have space in the kitchen for the bulkier items, keep them in a utility area.

GLASS AND BOTTLE CONTAINER
Make sure it's sturdy and leak-proof and rinse items before putting them in.

PLASTIC-BAG HOLDER
To save space, look out for one that's designed to be hung on the back of a cupboard door.

COMPOST CADDY
Collect food waste here and clean once a week to avoid flies and odours.

CONTAINER FOR CANS
Rinse cans before storing them. To save space, crush them with a can-crusher.

CONTAINER FOR PAPER
Use exclusively for dry items, such as paper and cardboard, to avoid them becoming soggy. Flatten boxes before putting them in.

15 MIN Living room speed-clean

Although the living room can easily get cluttered, fortunately the mess is usually superficial. It's nothing that 15 minutes with a damp cloth and a vacuum can't sort out. Make sure you vacuum last to collect dust dislodged during cleaning.

1 LET IN THE FRESH AIR
Open the window to let in some fresh air. You could also light a fragranced candle or use a naturally fragranced room-freshener spray.

2 GET RID OF CRUMBS
You may not have time to vacuum sofas and chairs, but at least remove any crumbs by scooping them up in a barely damp microfibre cloth.

3 TIDY AUDIOVISUAL EQUIPMENT
Put audiovisual equipment in its proper place. Don't leave CDs, DVDs, or games out of their boxes to gather dust.

4 WIPE THE TELEVISION
Use a barely damp microfibre cloth to remove any sticky fingerprints from the television screen.

5 STOW TOYS AWAY

Pile children's toys into a trunk or other large storage box and stow it in a corner. Wipe any grubby items with a damp microfibre cloth.

6 CLEAN THE MIRRORS

Use a barely damp microfibre cloth to clean any smears from the mirrors. Add a tiny drop of washing-up liquid for stubborn marks.

7 TIDY THE SURFACES

Take glasses and mugs back to the kitchen, put books back on book shelves, and put magazines in the magazine rack.

8 STRAIGHTEN THE FURNITURE

Straighten sofas, chairs, and rugs. If you have throws, fold them and arrange them neatly on the backs of chairs and sofas or on armrests.

9 DO A QUICK DUST

Use a damp microfibre cloth to quickly tackle dust hotspots, such as book shelves, photo frames, and lampshades.

10 FINISH BY VACUUMING

Vacuum the floor and rugs, focusing particularly on heavy-traffic areas like the doorway and in front of the sofa. If you have time, pull out the sofa and vacuum behind.

Clean a washable wall

Clean your walls regularly and you'll never have to deal with a hard-to-shift build-up of dirt. Use this speedy method just once a year. Start by vacuuming to remove surface dirt, then the job's less messy.

BARE ESSENTIALS

vacuum cleaner

dusting-brush attachment

bucket

washing-up liquid

large sponge, towel

→1

Before you start to wash, remove dust from the wall by vacuuming it with the dusting-brush attachment. Start at the top and work your way down.

→2

Fill a bucket with warm water and add a squirt of washing-up liquid. Wet the sponge in the water, then wring it out thoroughly so dirty drips don't streak the wall.

Extra tips

To clean a wallpapered wall, vacuum with the dusting-brush attachment (see step 1), then check if the paper is washable. To do this, carefully wet an inconspicuous area. If the colour bleeds or fades, then you'll have to stop and accept that you can only vacuum the paper. If it proves washable, proceed, following steps 2–4 below.

To remove heavy grease from a washable wall, for example from the area around a hob, make a solution of warm water and a handful of soda crystals. Wet a sponge in the solution, wring it out thoroughly, then use to wipe the wall. Rinse the sponge in clean water and wipe again to rinse off the solution. Repeat if necessary.

→3

Sponge the wall, starting at the top and working your way down. When one area is clean, rinse out your sponge and wipe the surface again to remove the detergent.

→4

Working as quickly as possible to avoid streaking, pat the wall dry using a towel. A very dirty wall might need a second clean once it has dried. If so, repeat steps 2–4.

5 MIN Clean a television

Like all electronic equipment, televisions generate static, which attracts dust – and dust can damage the components inside. It only takes a few minutes to dust and then clean the television too.

BARE ESSENTIALS

vacuum cleaner with dusting-brush attachment

microfibre cloths

washing-up liquid

Unplug the television, then use the dusting-brush attachment on your vacuum cleaner and vacuum the back, paying special attention to the ventilation grilles.

Using a wet microfibre cloth that has been squeezed out thoroughly, wipe away any dirt and dust on the television casing, the wires, and the plug.

WHAT TO DO WHEN

DAILY → Give the screen a quick wipe with a barely damp cloth to remove dust.

WEEKLY → Vacuum behind the television with the dusting-brush attachment.

MONTHLY → Wipe electronic equipment with a barely damp cloth. Include remote controls (see box, right), DVD players, and games' consoles.

Clean the remote control

Wipe with a damp cloth to remove dust. Make sure the cloth is well wrung out as you must avoid getting water inside.

Use a cotton bud squeezed out in warm water and a little washing-up liquid to remove any dirt from between the buttons.

→3

→4

Using another well-squeezed-out microfibre cloth with a dab of washing-up liquid, gently remove any dirty marks from the television screen.

Using a dry microfibre cloth with firm downward movements, gently buff the screen dry. Work quickly to avoid leaving streak marks on the screen.

10 MIN Polish wooden furniture

If you've got an old or special piece of solid-wood furniture, treat it carefully. This speedy wax will restore the shine and feed the wood. And the great thing is you only need to do it once or twice a year.

BARE ESSENTIALS

small, soft, decorator's paintbrush

microfibre cloths

beeswax furniture polish

duster

→1

First dislodge surface dust from any crevices or mouldings on the furniture. The best tool for doing this is a small, soft, decorator's paintbrush.

→2

Use a microfibre cloth to remove the rest of the dust. Make sure you have removed it all before applying polish or the dust will be ground into the wood with the polish.

WHAT TO DO WHEN

WEEKLY → Dry-dust (see pp.18–19) regularly to remove surface dust.

EVERY FEW MONTHS → If the surface is losing its gleam, buff it up gently using a clean duster, as in step 4.

HALF-YEARLY → Clean and polish once or twice a year by following steps 1–4 below.

Extra tips

To remove grease marks from wooden furniture, sprinkle the marks with talcum powder then cover with kitchen paper. Press down firmly and the paper will absorb the grease.

If damaged furniture is antique, don't repair it yourself, but take it to a specialist restorer. This will avoid devaluing it.

→3

Apply a small amount of beeswax furniture polish to a clean microfibre cloth, then apply to the furniture, wiping in the direction of the grain. Repeat as necessary.

→4

When you have applied a thin layer of wax to the whole surface, use a clean duster to gently buff it. The surface should have a soft gleam when you have finished.

Remove scratches from a solid-wood floor

10 MIN

Polishing a solid-wood floor is a major job that you should do once a year with a hired polishing machine. In between polishes, keep your floor scratch-free with this simple, speedy technique.

BARE ESSENTIALS

vacuum cleaner

hard-floor floorhead

fine steel wool (grade 000)

floor wax, spatula

duster

→1

As soon as possible after you have spotted the scratches, remove any furniture that is in the way, and vacuum the area thoroughly using the head for hard floors.

→2

Gently rub the scratches with fine steel wool (grade 000) until you can no longer see them. Sweep away the dust left behind with a dustpan and brush.

Extra tips

To remove chewing gum, candle wax, or wax crayon from a wooden floor, cover the area with an ice-filled plastic bag, leave until the gum or wax has hardened, then carefully remove, using a blunt knife or the edge of a plastic card like a credit card.

You can't sand scratches on a wood laminate floor as you can on a solid-wood floor because the surface of wood laminate often consists of nothing more than a photographic appliqué on top of a core of melamine and fibreboard. To remove scratches, use a special laminate repair kit.

To prevent scratches on wooden floors, always use cup castors on chair and table legs.

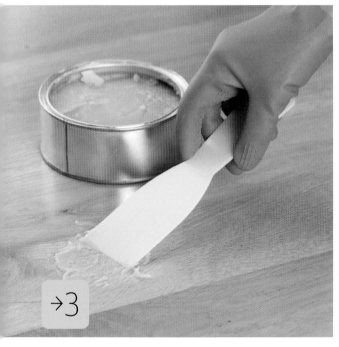

→3

Using a small spatula, carefully apply a little floor wax to the scratched area. Work the wax into the scratches by pressing on the spatula, Leave for 15 minutes.

→4

Using a clean duster, thoroughly buff the area. Turn the duster from time to time so you always use a clean part. Continue until you have a smooth, polished surface.

Vacuum a sofa

Sofas are expensive and crumbs and dirt will damage their covers. Keep them in tip-top condition by giving them a speedy vacuum every week. If you notice any stains, follow the stain-removal tips in Chapter 4.

BARE ESSENTIALS

vacuum cleaner

crevice nozzle

dusting-brush attachment

→1
Remove all cushions and seat cushions, and lay them on the floor. If your sofa stands next to the wall, pull it away so you can vacuum behind.

→2
Check between the back and seat and down the sides for any items that may have fallen there, then vacuum in all the nooks and crannies using the crevice nozzle.

Cleaning upholstered furniture

Clean upholstered furniture roughly once a year, depending on how much use it gets. Don't wait until it looks dirty: by then the dirt will have started to damage the fabric.

If your furniture has fitted covers, call in a professional. The job will be done more quickly and the results will be better thanks to the professional equipment.

If you have loose covers, follow the manufacturer's instructions. You can usually wash them on a cool wash at the launderette. Leave them to dry naturally to avoid shrinkage and put them back on the sofa while they're still damp – that way it's easier to get them back on.

→3

Using the dusting-brush attachment and gentle suction, vacuum the entire sofa, including the back and cushions. Focus especially on areas where dust gathers.

→4

When you have finished, replace the seat cushions, plump the loose cushions, and put them back on the sofa. Move the sofa back into position.

20 MIN Polish a leather sofa

Although you should wipe up spills immediately and vacuum crumbs each week, a leather sofa only needs a proper clean and polish once a year. Use soft saddle soap to do both jobs at the same time.

BARE ESSENTIALS

vacuum with dusting-brush attachment

microfibre cloths

soft saddle soap

dry sponge

duster

→1

Check down the sides of the sofa for any items that have fallen there, then vacuum the whole surface using the soft dusting-brush attachment.

→2

Wet a microfibre cloth in warm water and squeeze it out thoroughly so it is barely damp. Use this to wipe away any remaining surface dirt.

Extra tips

You can polish the leather with a leather-conditioner spray, but note that these only polish. They don't clean.

To remove water-based stains, dab them immediately with a soft white cloth or kitchen paper. Leave to dry thoroughly and if the mark's still visible, buff the area with a clean dry cloth.

To remove greasy stains, treat with a solution of soap flakes or use soft saddle soap, then rinse with clear water. Always make sure you don't overwet the leather.

→3

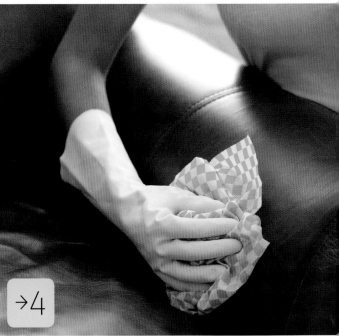

→4

To remove ingrained dirt and nourish the leather at the same time, apply soft saddle soap on a dry sponge, working on a small area at a time. Rub in the saddle soap well.

Finish by rubbing the entire surface of the sofa with a clean, dry microfibre cloth. Use a firm repetitive motion to bring a glow to the leather.

Polishing kit

The polishing kit you need depends on the items you've got to polish. Traditional beeswax polish is best for wooden furniture and floors. Silicone polishes don't fill small scratches as beeswax does, and it can make surfaces slippery. Brass, copper, and silver ornaments need a quick polish from time to time to keep tarnish at bay.

MICROFIBRE MITT
Use a mitt rather than a cloth for quickly dusting large surfaces like tables and cupboard fronts. Microfibre can be machine-washed but don't use fabric conditioner.

METAL POLISH
Some products suit several different metals, but check before use.

MICROFIBRE CLOTHS
Use to remove dust quickly and efficiently before you start to polish. Microfibre is electrostatic so it attracts dust like a magnet

DUSTER
The traditional soft cloth used for dusting. Now there are microfibre cloths, you may prefer to save it just for buffing up surfaces after polishing.

DECORATOR'S BRUSH
A handy tool for getting rid of surface dust from mouldings on furniture.

TOOTHBRUSH
Use an old one to ease dust out of mouldings and intricate details on ornaments.

OLD TOWEL
Use when polishing small items to protect the surface you're working on from the polish, which may damage it.

BEESWAX POLISH
This is the gentlest wax for feeding and shining solid wood. You only need to apply it once or twice a year.

RUBBER GLOVES
Always wear gloves when polishing furniture and metals to protect your hands from the polish.

15 MIN Bedroom speed-clean

Keep your bedroom and dressing table fresh and tidy. Run through this speed-clean checklist at least once a week, and you'll cover every aspect of the room, from the bed to the waste bin and from the mirrors to the floor.

1 LET IN THE FRESH AIR
Even in winter, let some air into the bedroom by opening a window. This will help to keep it smelling fresh, and will reduce humidity and keep it cool, both of which deter dust mites.

2 AIR THE BED
Try to air the bed first thing every morning. When you get up, turn the duvet or top sheet and blankets back over the foot of the bed.

3 DAMP-DUST
Wipe washable surfaces with a damp cloth, particularly bedside tables, where dust may have gathered around lamps, books, and other items.

4 MAKE THE BED
When the bed has aired for at least 30 minutes, make the bed and plump the pillows. If you have a bedspread, throw it over for that hotel-bedroom look.

5 **CLEAN THE MIRRORS**
If mirrors are smeared, wipe them clean with a barely damp microfibre cloth. If stubborn marks remain, repeat, adding a tiny drop of washing-up liquid to the cloth.

6 **RETURN ITEMS TO THE CORRECT ROOM**
Remove mugs or other kitchen items that have found their way into the bedroom, along with anything else that doesn't belong there.

7 **EMPTY THE WASTE BIN**
Empty the waste bin, separating any items that can be recycled and putting the rest with the household rubbish. Line with a clean liner.

8 **PUT CLOTHES AWAY**
Sort out clothes that are lying around, putting like with like, then shake them out and hang them up in the wardrobe, or fold and place in the drawer.

9 **STOW COSMETICS AND OTHER PERSONAL ITEMS**
Store items away neatly in covered baskets or bowls to minimize dusting. Remember that anything left on show will only gather dust.

10 **FINISH BY VACUUMING**
Focus on areas where there is heavy traffic, like the doorway and alongside the bed. Use the crevice nozzle in the corners. If there's time, pull out the bed and vacuum behind.

Change the bed

4 MIN

Change your bedlinen once a week – and more frequently in hot weather. There's no need to struggle to put on duvet covers and pillowcases if you follow these simple steps.

BARE ESSENTIALS

bed

duvet and duvet cover

fitted bottom sheet

pillows and pillowcases

→1

Remove the dirty bedding and pile the duvet and pillows nearby. Pull on a clean fitted bottom sheet, pull it tight over the corners, and smooth out any wrinkles.

→2

Turn a pillowcase inside out, reach into the corners, grab the corners of a pillow, then roll the pillowcase down over the pillow. Arrange the pillows on the bed.

Extra tips

Duvets are easier to look after than blankets and you can make the bed in moments. The main choice is between down, feather and down, and synthetic fillings. Goose down is the best insulator but is more expensive. Down is sometimes combined with duck feathers to reduce the cost. Synthetic fillings – usually polyester hollowfibre – are best for allergy sufferers.

Most duvets with natural fillings must be professionally laundered, but you can launder duvets with a synthetic filling yourself (see pp.148–9).

Pillows come with the same fillings as duvets. In addition, you can buy latex-filled pillows, which keep their shape well and are good for people with allergies.

→3

→4

Lay the duvet cover on the bed. Push a corner of the duvet into a top corner of the cover, do the same with the other corner. Now pull the cover down.

When the duvet is fully inside the cover, hold the cover and the duvet together, and shake the duvet flat. Fasten the bottom opening of the duvet cover.

2 MIN Make the bed

Get into the habit of making your bed every morning as soon as you get up. It only takes a minute or two – excluding airing time – and will freshen up the bed, helping to get rid of dust mites and flakes of dead skin that you have shed during the night.

→1

→2

As soon as you get up, fold the duvet back on itself and lay it at the foot of the bed. Leave it so that it airs while you get washed and ready for the day.

At least 30 minutes later, dust the bottom sheet with your hand and smooth it down. Fit it back tightly over the corners of the mattress, then tuck it in well at the sides.

Extra tips

If you have blankets and a flat bottom sheet, start by following step 1 below, and air the bed by folding back the blankets and the top sheet instead of the duvet. Now smooth the bottom sheet. Next, unfold the blankets and the top sheet, keeping them together, then fold back the top edge of the sheet. Move to the bottom of the bed. Tuck the sheets and blankets in firmly along the bottom, then lift the sides (again keeping sheets and blankets together) and fold them back on top of the bed. You'll now see a corner hanging down. Tuck this in, then drop the sides back down and tuck those in. You should now have a neat mitre – a hospital corner.

→3

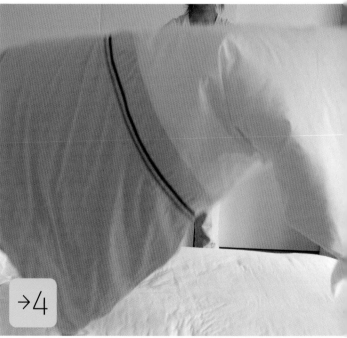

→4

Plump up the pillows as these will have been flattened in the night. Lay them neatly at the head of the bed, turning them round so last night's top edge is at the bottom.

Finally, use a brisk upward motion to shake the duvet and let it fall back onto the bed. Now straighten the duvet out, making sure it covers the bed evenly.

10 MIN Maintain your mattress

Vacuum your mattress every six months, sponge off stains and, if it's a sprung mattress, turn it over. These simple steps will extend the life of the mattress by years and will keep dust mites at bay.

BARE ESSENTIALS

vacuum cleaner

dusting-brush attachment

handwash laundry detergent

sponge

→1

Remove the mattress protector then vacuum the mattress using the dusting-brush attachment. Work the brush well into the stitching to help remove dust mites.

→2

Squeeze out a sponge in a solution of warm water and handwash laundry detergent and use to scrub away stains. Sponge with clean water to remove the detergent.

Extra tips

Always use a mattress protector on top of your mattress as it's more hygienic. Launder it – together with pillow protectors (another essential) – monthly.

As well as turning a sprung mattress over, you should also turn it from end to end. Turn it over every 6 months and from end to end after another 6 months.

You don't have to turn latex and memory-foam mattresses over, but you should still rotate them from end to end to maximise their lifespan. Do this once a month.

To combat the smell from any urine stains, dab the stains with a 1:4 solution of white vinegar to water. Finish by dabbing with a clean, dry cloth.

→3

→4

Leave the mattress to dry, then turn it over. If you want to speed up the drying process, use a warm hairdryer. Vacuum the other side and sponge off stains there too.

When the second side has dried, replace the mattress protector with a clean one. You are now ready to make the bed again, following steps 1–4 on pp.78–9.

Bathroom kit

Keeping the bathroom clean is important for hygiene reasons. Clean mess up quickly before you leave the bathroom and you'll only have to spend a few minutes a week washing the floor and changing the towels. You don't need an extensive cleaning kit, but do keep it separate from the cleaning materials you use in the rest of the house.

TOILET CLEANER
The angled neck on the bottle makes it quicker and easier to squirt the cleaner inside of the toilet, particularly under the rim of the pan.

KITCHEN TOWEL
Useful for wiping the exterior of the toilet; it's hygienic as you can throw the paper away afterwards.

SPRAY CLEANER
The spray speeds up the job of disinfecting the exterior of the toilet pan.

CREAM CLEANER
Use to quickly remove most marks from the bath and basin.

BATHROOM SPONGE
The abrasive side deals speedily with stubborn marks on the sink, bath, and shower.

VINEGAR SOLUTION
Spray in the sink, bath, and around the shower, to prevent limescale.

RUBBER GLOVES
Reserve a special pair for cleaning the toilet.

Bathroom speed-clean

5 MIN

You can achieve this bathroom speed-clean in just 5 minutes if you gather the appropriate cleaning materials in a washing-up bowl before you start work. Keep this tool kit ready in a bathroom cupboard for future use.

1 VENTILATE THE ROOM
Either open a window or turn the extractor fan on while you follow the rest of the steps. Good ventilation stops damp and mildew.

2 WIPE THE SINK
Using a barely damp cloth, wipe behind the taps and around the sink to remove any soap scum. Empty and wipe the soap dish if it's full of soapy water.

3 WIPE THE BATH
Using a barely damp cloth, wipe the bath to remove soap scum, hair, and other dirt. Wipe up water from behind the taps and remove hair from the plughole.

4 DRY THE SHOWER CURTAIN OR SCREEN
If the shower curtain's wet, open it fully, shake it out, wipe it dry, and leave it open. If you have a shower screen, wipe it dry.

5 CLEAN THE TOILET

Wipe the seat with a piece of kitchen towel, then spray or squirt disinfectant toilet cleaner into the bowl, especially around the rim. Once a week, clean the outside of the bowl and the handle.

6 CLEAN THE MIRRORS

Clean any smears from the mirrors using a barely damp microfibre cloth. If there are stubborn marks, remove them with a tiny drop of washing-up liquid.

7 TIDY THE TOILETRIES

Store like with like, putting as many items as possible away in the bathroom cabinet or in drawers. If you leave them out on display, they'll gather dust.

8 CHANGE TOWELS AND FLANNELS

Once a week, replace dirty towels and flannels with clean ones. If you have a full machine load, wash them straight away, but if not and they're not dry, leave to dry before putting in the laundry bin.

9 CLEAN THE FLOOR

Sweep the floor to remove dust and fluff. At least once a week, mop with a floor-cleaning product, focusing on the area around the toilet.

10 EMPTY THE WASTE BIN

Empty the waste bin, separating any items that can be recycled and putting the rest with the household rubbish. Line with a clean liner.

3 MIN Clean the bathroom sink

Bathroom sinks get a lot of use and can harbour germs. This deep-clean only takes minutes. Get into the habit of doing it after every use, and you won't need to spend any time cleaning the sink more thoroughly.

BARE ESSENTIALS

double-sided bathroom sponge

cream cleaner

spray bottle

white vinegar

microfibre cloth

→1

Clear clutter from around the sink, then fill with hot water and leave for a minute to loosen any soap scum. Wipe the sink with the sponge, then let the water drain away.

→2

Use the abrasive side of the sponge and some cream cleaner to remove any marks, especially from the plughole, the overflow, and around the base of the taps. Rinse well.

WHAT TO DO WHEN

DAILY → Wipe the sink down after every use to keep it free of soap scum.

WEEKLY → Give the sink and taps a thorough clean following steps 1–4.

MONTHLY → If there's a limescale build-up, soak kitchen towel in white vinegar, lay it on the limescale, and leave until the limescale is soft and you can wipe it away.

Extra tips

Clean a stone sink with a soft cloth and a neutral or alkaline cleaning product. Use a specialised stone-cleaning product for persistent stains, and to prevent stains, use a stone-sealant once a year.

Use an old toothbrush to clean hard-to-reach areas such as behind the taps.

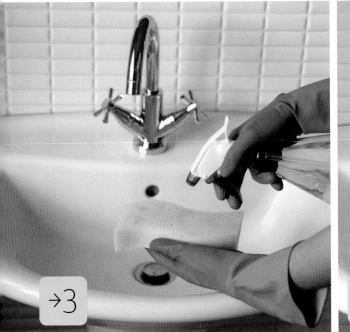

To minimise any build-up of limescale, mix equal parts of white vinegar and water. Spray the solution onto the sponge, wipe around the sink and taps, then rinse.

For a sparkling finish, dry the sink with a clean, dry microfibre cloth. Use this to polish the taps and plughole too. Drying helps to prevent limescale deposits.

Clean the bath

5 MIN

Take a few moments to wipe the bath out after every use, then you'll only need minutes for this weekly clean. If you wait till there's an old, dried-on tidemark, it will take a lot longer to restore the bath's sparkle.

BARE ESSENTIALS

double-sided bathroom sponge

cream cleaner

spray bottle

white vinegar

microfibre cloth

→1

Using a damp sponge, wipe around the bath to pick up soap, hair, and other dirt. Wipe away water that has collected on the edge of the bath or behind the taps. Rinse well.

→2

Apply cream cleaner to any stains or marks, using the abrasive side of the sponge. Leave the cleaner to work for 10 minutes then rinse well.

Extra tips

If your bath's been neglected and is badly stained, fill it with hot water, add a scoop of laundry detergent, and leave it overnight. The next day, let the water out, then wipe around with a sponge. The stains and soap scum should disappear.

To clean mould from the sealant round the bath, use a fungicidal spray. Once the sealant's clean, reapply it regularly to prevent the mould from reappearing.

To remove scratches from an acrylic bath, rub gently with metal polish then follow with a clean. Never use an abrasive cleaner or an abrasive sponge as these will scratch the surface.

→3

To prevent a build-up of limescale, mix equal parts of white vinegar and water. Spray the solution onto the sponge and wipe the entire bath, including the taps.

→4

Rinse the bath thoroughly, then finish by wiping the taps and any other chrome parts. First use the soft side of the sponge, then polish with a dry microfibre cloth.

5 MIN
Clean the shower

The main enemy of showers and shower cubicles is limescale, but you don't have to use a branded product to wage war. Keep it under control in just a few minutes a week with this simple, eco-friendly routine.

BARE ESSENTIALS

double-sided bathroom sponge

spray bottle

white vinegar

microfibre cloth

→1

→2

Start by wiping down the walls and floor of the shower cubicle using the soft side of a damp bathroom sponge. Be sure to wipe away any pools of water.

Mix equal parts of white vinegar and water in a spray bottle and use to spray the shower head and any other metal parts. Rinse, then polish with a dry microfibre cloth.

Extra tips

To keep a shower curtain clean, wash it regularly on a hot wash using biological detergent. If it's badly mildewed, soak it for 10 minutes in a solution of 1 part household bleach to 4 parts water before you machine-wash. Alternatively, scrub the mildew with a paste made from bicarbonate of soda and water, then rinse in plenty of clean water. A final solution if the curtain's heavily mildewed is to spray it with a branded mildew remover, following the manufacturer's instructions.

To clean mould and mildew from grouting, scrub with a solution of 1 part bleach to 3 parts water or with a paste made from bicarbonate of soda with a couple of drops of white vinegar or bleach.

→3

→4

Next tackle the door to remove smears and any build-up of limescale. Do this by spraying with the vinegar-and-water spray, then rinse with a damp sponge.

Finish by drying the door using a clean, dry microfibre cloth. Work quickly to avoid streaking. If the door has any metal trim or a metal handle, dry those too.

Clean the toilet

3 MIN

Toilets are breeding grounds for bacteria. Destroy them with this speedy, weekly clean. If several people use the toilet, also clean it daily with a squirt of branded toilet cleaner from an angle-necked bottle.

BARE ESSENTIALS

disinfectant toilet cleaner

kitchen towel

toilet brush

spray bottle

white vinegar

→1

Spray a disinfectant toilet cleaner around the inside and outside of the toilet pan. Leave the inside to soak for a few minutes while you wipe outside with kitchen towel.

→2

Clean the pan with the toilet brush, especially under the rim. Flush the toilet and while it is flushing, use the brush to rinse away any remaining disinfectant.

Extra tips

To remove a heavy build-up of limescale in the toilet, remove most of the water from the pan using a plastic cup (see step 2, p. 96), then pour in white vinegar to cover the stains. Leave until the stain has gone, then flush to wash the vinegar away. Alternatively, use a branded limescale-removing product, following the manufacturer's instructions.

You can use household bleach inside the pan as an alternative disinfectant, but don't leave it to soak for more than 30 minutes to avoid damaging the porcelain.

Never mix different toilet-cleaning products. They contain chemicals that may react together to produce toxic gases.

→3

To prevent limescale or treat a mild build-up, mix equal parts of white vinegar and water in a spray. Spray generously in the toilet pan and leave to soak for 10 minutes.

→4

Flush the toilet one more time to wash away the vinegar. Finish by giving the seat a final wipe with a piece of kitchen towel to soak up any splashes.

<table>
<tr><td>10
MIN</td></tr>
</table>

Unblock a toilet

When your toilet gets blocked, try to stay calm and see if the blockage clears itself. If it doesn't, put on your rubber gloves, gather your tools together (see box, right), and set about using this speedy remedy.

BARE ESSENTIALS

newspaper

plastic cup

bucket

plunger

bleach

→1

Lay newspaper down around the toilet pan to protect the floor from any splashes. Start by trying to pull out any visible obstruction with your hands.

→2

If that doesn't unblock the toilet, you'll have to use a plunger. Begin by emptying most of the water from the toilet pan using a plastic cup. Pour the water into a bucket.

Extra tips

When you're faced with a blocked toilet, you often have the urge to keep on flushing the toilet in the hope that this will clear the blockage. It won't. You'll simply end up with a flooded floor.

Avoid a blocked toilet in the first place by only throwing toilet paper in the pan.

Never try and flush disposable nappies, tissues, sanitary towels, or tampons. Also, train everyone in the household to only use small quantities of toilet paper with each flush. Even an excess of toilet paper can cause a blockage.

If all else fails, call a plumber.

→3

→4

Place the plunger tightly over the toilet outlet. Press it down firmly, then quickly lift it up and press it down. You may need to pump up and down like this up to 10 times.

When the blockage has cleared and the water level has fallen, flush the toilet, then squirt a small amount of bleach around the rim to disinfect the pan.

5 MIN Home office speed-clean

Whether your home office is a desk in your bedroom or an entire room, it will need regular attention to keep the area uncluttered and dust-free. Follow these steps once a week and you'll feel much more on top of your work space.

1 BRING IN THE FRESH AIR
Open windows to bring in some fresh air or if that's not possible, light a fragranced candle or use a naturally fragranced room-freshener spray.

2 RETURN ITEMS TO THE CORRECT ROOM
If there are empty coffee cups or plates around your desk, take them to the kitchen. Return stray items from other rooms to their rightful places.

3 TIDY THE DESK AREA
Before you can dust and clean your desk, you need to tidy it. Put paperwork in a pile ready to file, put books and magazines on shelves, and tidy away pens, pencils, notebooks, and other bits and pieces.

4 CLEAN THE DESK
Using a damp cloth and a squirt of all-purpose cleaner, wipe around the desk to remove any sticky marks or stains.

5 SPEED-CLEAN THE KEYBOARD
Tip the keyboard upside down and shake out the dust and crumbs, then wipe with a barely damp microfibre cloth to remove dirt and grubby fingerprint marks.

6 CLEAN THE COMPUTER SCREEN
Using a dry microfibre cloth, give the screen a quick buff and remove any dust that has collected on or around it.

7 WIPE THE PHONE
Wipe the phone with a barely damp microfibre cloth and at least once a month, dampen a cloth with disinfectant spray and wipe the handset.

8 TIDY LEADS AND CABLES
Check that leads and cables are tucked away along the skirting board or behind your desk, and that they're not cluttering up the desk area.

9 CLEAN THE CHAIR
Wipe your office chair with a damp cloth to pick up any hair and surface dirt. If there are stains, spend a moment tackling them with an upholstery-cleaning product.

10 FINISH BY VACUUMING
Vacuum the floor, focusing on heavy-traffic areas such as the doorway and the area under your desk.

10 MIN Clean a laptop

A laptop quickly gathers crumbs, hair, dust, and dirt. These harbour bacteria and could affect the laptop's performance. This clean only takes minutes and will keep your laptop in good working order.

BARE ESSENTIALS

microfibre cloths

spray can of compressed air

cotton buds

→1

Unplug the laptop before you begin and remove any peripherals. Close the lid then wipe the outer casing with a barely damp microfibre cloth.

→2

Open the laptop then, from about 15 cm (6 in) away, carefully spray compressed air around the keyboard, air vents, ports, and CD/DVD slot.

BEFORE YOU BEGIN

TURN OFF THE LAPTOP AND UNPLUG IT
→ Water and electricity don't mix!

DON'T RUSH → Hurry at your peril. You risk causing damage.

REMOVE ALL PERIPHERALS → These include the mouse, printer cable, keyboard cable, and anything plugged into a port or slot.

Extra tips

If you don't have a can of compressed air, use a hairdryer on its coolest setting to blow dust away from air vents and from the keyboard.

You could also use a soft paintbrush for dislodging dust, and anti-static wipes for cleaning the screen.

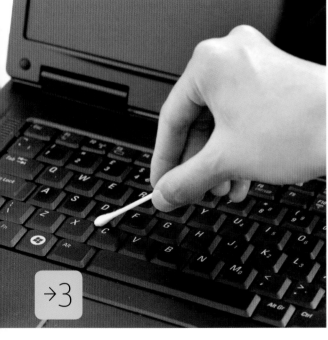

→3

Dampen a cotton bud in warm water, squeeze it well and use between the keys to remove marks and dirt. Finish by wiping with a barely damp microfibre cloth.

→4

Using a dry microfibre cloth, wipe surface dust off the screen, then dampen the cloth very slightly and wipe again. Finish by buffing with a clean, dry cloth.

Washing up

Washing-up kit

If you don't have a dishwasher or are trying to cut down on using yours, then you'll have to wash up by hand. But you don't want to spend ages doing it. The speedy way to get a stack of clean dishes is to use the right kit, and here is what you need. Keep it all to hand near the sink, and you'll whizz through the washing up in a trice.

DOUBLE-SIDED SPONGES
Be sure to use a non-scratch sponge on non-stick pans.

SOAP-DISPENSING SCOURER
Fill the handle with washing-up liquid and you have a quick and easy way of washing up when you've only got one or two dirty items.

CUTLERY DRAINER
Stand one on your draining rack to hold cutlery after it has been washed. For safety, put knives blade-end down, but forks and spoons dry better handle-end down.

TEA TOWELS
Wash regularly on a hot wash and use a clean one for every batch of washing up.

WASHING-UP BOWL
Useful to avoid scratching your sink and for washing up glasses.

SCOURERS
These quickly remove most burnt-on food. Choose a plastic scourer to clean a non-stick pan.

WASHING-UP LIQUID
Don't use too much: a squirt is all you need for a sinkful of water.

WASHING-UP BRUSH
Use to clean food from the tines of forks. Be sure to give it a good hot wash from time to time.

DRAINING RACK
Save drying-up time by air-drying your dishes on a rack standing on the draining board.

SPONGE
Use to clean glassware.

RUBBER GLOVES
Always wear these to stop your hands drying out as you wash up.

4 MIN Prepare to wash up

Washing up doesn't have to be horribly time-consuming. For speed and efficiency, spend a minute or two setting things up first. And remember that you need clean tools for the job and plenty of hot water.

> **BARE ESSENTIALS**
>
> washing-up liquid
>
> sponge
>
> washing-up brush
>
> pan scourer or non-scratch sponge

→1

→2

Fill food-encrusted pans with enough hot water to cover the food. Add a squirt of washing-up liquid and leave to soak while you carry on with the rest of the preparation.

Clear the draining board and sink of clutter by removing any dirty dishes that have been piled in the sink or any clean items left on the draining rack.

BEFORE YOU BEGIN

IF YOU CAN'T WASH UP STRAIGHT AWAY
→ Rinse items so the dirt doesn't harden.

DON'T POUR OILS AND FATS DOWN THE SINK → They'll block it. Instead, pour into an old jar, and when it's full, throw it away.

SOAK PROTEIN DEBRIS LIKE EGG, MILK, AND PORRIDGE IN COLD WATER →These respond better to a soak in cold water than in hot.

Loading the dishwasher

Scrape off large food particles and unless dishes are only lightly soiled, rinse quickly before loading. They'll emerge cleaner and it helps avoid nasty smells while you wait for a full load.

Load matching items near each other. It makes for faster unloading and putting away.

Scrape food from the plates into the bin and stack the dirty dishes on the counter by the sink, roughly in the order that they will be washed (see pp.108–9).

Fill one sink with hot water and add a squirt of washing-up liquid. Fill a second sink or washing-up bowl with hot water ready for rinsing the clean dishes.

10 MIN Do the washing up

The quickest way is to start with cleaner, delicate items and move onto heavier, dirtier ones. That way, the water stays cleaner for longer. As you work, check that every item is clean before you move on to the next.

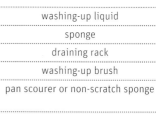

BARE ESSENTIALS

washing-up liquid

sponge

draining rack

washing-up brush

pan scourer or non-scratch sponge

→1

→2

Start by washing the glassware with a sponge. Be gentle to avoid breakages, then dip in the hot rinsing water and place, bottom up, on the draining rack.

Next wash the cleanest plates, followed by the dirtier ones. Change the water if it gets oily. Use a washing-up brush, then rinse in the hot water before draining.

ACTION PLAN

BEFORE YOU START → Really hot water gives best results, so wearing gloves is a must.

AS YOU WORK → Change the water when it gets oily, especially when you're washing up a big load.

AFTERWARDS → Rinse the sink with hot water and a drop of washing-up liquid.

Extra tips

Air-dry The best method of drying the washing-up is to leave items on a draining rack or on the draining board.

Towel-dry If you prefer to use a tea towel, make sure it's clean to avoid spreading bacteria onto your clean dishes and cutlery.

→3

→4

Now move on to the cutlery. Use the washing-up brush to make sure you clean all the food off the tines of the forks. Dip in the hot rinsing water and leave to drain.

Scrub pots and pans with a pan scourer or a non-scratch sponge if you are cleaning a non-stick pan. Rinse each item in hot water before standing it on the rack to drain.

10 MIN Make glasses sparkle

Glasses often develop a white haze in the dishwasher. If the glass has been "etched" – slightly dissolved by alkaline detergent – it's irreversible. If it's just limescale deposit, the acid in vinegar will help remove it.

BARE ESSENTIALS

washing-up liquid

rinsing bowl

white vinegar

sponge

draining rack

→1

→2

Fill a sink with hot water and a drop of washing-up liquid, and a second sink or a washing up bowl with white vinegar and water (1:8). Fill a third bowl with hot water.

Wash one glass at a time in the soapy water, using a sponge. Pay special attention to the rim of the glass where smudges and marks build up.

BEFORE YOU BEGIN

PUT ON RUBBER GLOVES → That way you can use really hot water, which will get your glasses cleaner.

USE A PLASTIC BOWL → If glasses are precious or delicate, it prevents damage.

USE A LARGE BOWL FOR THE VINEGAR SOLUTION → You must be able to roll your largest glass in it.

Extra tip

Borax is another all-round cleaner that produces good results on glassware but without the vinegary smell. Make a solution of 1 teaspoon of borax to 1 litre (1¾ pints) of hot water, then follow the instructions below, using the borax solution in step 3. Be sure to rinse well, borax shouldn't be ingested.

→3

→4

Now roll each glass in the bowl containing the vinegar solution. Dip the top of the glass in first, then the bottom, or stem, if it's a wine glass.

Finally, rinse the glass in the hot water to remove the vinegar. Stand it bottom up on a draining rack or on a clean tea towel on the draining board.

Pan-maintenance kit

Keep pans in tip-top condition by always cleaning them straight after use. That way there won't be a build-up of dirt and grease that takes ages to shift. Most dirty pans can be cleaned in a minute or two if you have the right equipment. When you're faced with burnt-on food, simply leave the pans to soak for a while.

WASHING-UP LIQUID
Your first defence against greasy pans. Today's products cut through grease fast.

THIN CLOTHS
Useful for placing between non-stick pans when they're stacked on top of each other in a cupboard.

SCOURER
Use to clean stainless-steel pans after you've soaked them in some soapy water.

BICARBONATE OF SODA
A good eco-friendly alternative to using chemical cleaning products.

MICROFIBRE CLOTHS
Use to remove greasy marks from the outside of stainless-steel pans.

KITCHEN TOWEL
A very quick (occasional) cheat for cleaning non-stick pans when they're only lightly soiled.

LEMON JUICE
Used with salt, it's a quick and eco-friendly way of cleaning copper pans.

RUBBER GLOVES
Wear rubber gloves when cleaning pans to protect your hands.

SALT
Use with lemon juice for cleaning tarnish from copper pans.

5 MIN Clean a burnt pan

When you have to deal with food that's stuck to the bottom of a saucepan, don't waste time trying to scrape it off. The job will only take minutes if you soak the pan as soon as possible.

BARE ESSENTIALS

wooden spoon

bicarbonate of soda

scourer

washing-up liquid

washing-up brush

→1

Scrape loose bits of food into the compost bin or into an ordinary bin. Use a wooden spoon or spatula, or a plastic spatula if it's a non-stick pan.

→2

Sprinkle some bicarbonate of soda onto the burnt-on food, then add enough hot water to cover the dirty areas. Leave to soak for at least an hour.

BEFORE YOU BEGIN

PUT ON RUBBER GLOVES → These will protect your hands at every stage.

REMOVE ANY WOODEN UTENSILS → Don't leave the pan to soak with a wooden spoon in it as the spoon might swell and crack.

CHECK YOUR MATERIALS → Avoid using metal scourers or harsh abrasive cleaning detergent on a non-stick pan.

Extra tip

After you have removed any loose bits of food (see step 1 opposite), pour a little laundry detergent in the pan. Half-fill with cold water, bring to the boil, and simmer for 15 minutes or until the burnt-on food loosens. Then remove it with a spoon or spatula, rinse, and dry.

→3

Using a metal scourer or a plastic one if it's a non-stick pan, work to dislodge the remaining burnt-on food. You should find that all the debris comes away.

→4

Discard the debris, then wash the pan as normal, using hot water, a squirt of washing-up liquid, and a washing-up brush. Leave the pan to dry.

10 TIPS

Using a dishwasher

There's nothing more frustrating than finding grubby items in the dishwasher after a wash. A dishwasher works like a shower. Its fixed jets only spray the surfaces they can reach. That's why how you stack items affects how well they're washed.

1 AVOID RINSING

There's no need to rinse items before loading unless food has dried on them. In this case, rinse to soften the food, then scrub it off. Otherwise, just scrape food off into the bin.

2 PUT THE RIGHT ITEM ON THE RIGHT RACK

Items on the lower rack get a hotter, more intense wash, so put heavily soiled things here, including pots and pans. Stack glassware, cups, and more delicate items on the top rack.

3 LOAD CUTLERY CORRECTLY

Load with some handles facing upwards and some down. This stops cutlery nestling together, which may mean it doesn't get so clean. Some dishwashers have cutlery shelves that prevent this from happening.

4 AVOID ITEMS TOUCHING

The idea is to load as much as you can without the items touching, or there's a risk they won't get clean. And always check that the spray arm at the bottom is free to rotate.

5 CHECK ITEMS ARE DISHWASHER-PROOF

Don't put rubber utensils, many non-stick pans, anything with a printed or painted pattern, and wooden items such as spoons and chopping boards in the dishwasher. These should be hand-washed.

6 TOP UP THE RINSE AID

Keep the rinse-aid compartment topped up. A small amount of rinse aid is released during the final hot rinse to help reduce smears.

7 AVOID WASHING TOO HOT

There's no need to choose the hottest cycle. It will cost you and the environment more and can damage glassware. For hygienic cleaning, all you need is a wash that's at least 52°C (126°F).

8 RINSE THE FILTER

Most new dishwashers have self-cleaning filters but if you have an older model, you may need to remove and rinse the filter regularly to get rid of food debris. Check the manufacturer's instructions.

9 TOP UP THE SALT

Even if your dishwasher tablets contain salt, you still need to top up the reservoir with granular salt every month, especially if you live in a hard-water area. The salt activates the machine's water softener.

10 RUN A MAINTENANCE WASH

Every couple of months, run a hot wash with an empty machine and a dishwasher-cleaning product. This removes grease and limescale from all parts of the dishwasher, including those you can't see.

3 MIN Make a sink sparkle

The kitchen sink's a prime breeding ground for bacteria, so give it a deep, disinfecting clean at least once a week. Always wear rubber gloves to do this job, to avoid splashing bleach on your skin.

BARE ESSENTIALS

bleach

old toothbrush

non-scratch sponge

→1

Make sure the sink area is free of dishes, then fill the sink with hot water until it's almost overflowing. Add a capful of bleach and leave to soak for a few minutes.

→2

The overflow is where dirt often collects. Splash a little of the bleach solution down the overflow then scrub it thoroughly using an old toothbrush.

WHAT TO DO WHEN

DAILY → Wipe the sink after every use, especially around the taps and the overflow.

WEEKLY → Follow steps 1–4 below to disinfect the sink thoroughly.

MONTHLY → Put your washing-up brushes and scourers in the bleach solution to disinfect them, or throw them out and replace them.

Extra tips

For porcelain sinks, swap the bleach solution for warm soapy water to avoid dulling the surface, and rub any stains with bicarbonate of soda.

If you use a washing-up bowl, wipe it with a sponge soaked in the bleach solution every week, when you give the sink a thorough clean.

→3

→4

With the bleach solution still in the sink, scrub away any stains on the sink using a non-scratch sponge. Stains most often form around the plughole.

Leave to soak for 1 hour or overnight, then let the water out of the sink. Rinse the sink thoroughly to be sure you remove all traces of bleach.

5 MIN Clear a slow-draining sink

A slow-draining kitchen sink is a sign of a blocked pipe. The most likely causes are grease, fat, and food debris. It usually only takes a few minutes to solve the problem and you shouldn't need chemicals.

BARE ESSENTIALS

bicarbonate of soda

white vinegar

plunger

bleach

→1 **Start by sprinkling** 80–100 g (3–3½ oz) bicarbonate of soda down the plughole, then wash it down with 240 ml (8½fl oz) boiling water.

→2 **If the blockage persists,** pour 80–100 ml (3–3½fl oz) white vinegar down the plughole, then flush with a full kettle of boiling water.

WHAT TO DO WHEN

DAILY → Clean any food debris from the plughole and rinse well.

WEEKLY → Pour a full kettle of boiling water down the plughole to prevent a build-up of debris in the waste pipe.

MONTHLY → Pour a cupful of white vinegar down the plughole to dissolve minor blockages.

Extra tips

Another way of dissolving grease is with soda crystals. Pour two cups of soda crystals over the plughole then slowly pour in a kettle of boiling water.

If all these methods fail, try a chemical drain-unblocking product. Remember that these are caustic, so wear rubber gloves and rinse the sink well afterwards.

Make sure there's 2½–5 cm (1–2 in) water in the sink, then cover the plughole with a plunger. Pressing down firmly, pump up and down several times.

When the blockage has cleared, rinse the sink and disinfect it with a little bleach. If the problem remains, try a drain-clearing chemical or call the plumber.

Clothes and laundry

5 MIN Sort the laundry

The key to avoiding laundry disasters is to sort your washing rigorously according to the manufacturer's care labels (see opposite). Some items are made of several fabrics and may include zips or buttons. The recommendation on the care label takes this into account.

→1

→2

Start by removing from the laundry basket any items labelled as handwash only. These will include silk, fine linen, some woollen items, and special lingerie.

Divide the remaining laundry firstly according to the care label, then according to colour. Make different piles for whites, dark colours, and bright colours.

LAUNDRY CARE LABELS

 WASH The numeral indicates the maximum temperature for washing.

 WASH A line underneath indicates the need for reduced agitation.

 HANDWASH If no temperature is specified, keep it low or cold.

 DRY CLEAN Letters in the circle indicate the type of dry-cleaning agent.

 DRY FLAT Lay on a towel on a flat surface or on a mesh rack over the bath.

DO NOT TUMBLE DRY These garments may not be tumble-dried safely.

DO NOT BLEACH If there's no cross, you can use any type of bleach.

 COOL IRON One, two, or three dots indicates the ironing temperature.

DO NOT IRON A cross indicates that ironing is not safe for this fabric.

→3

Make sure that you empty pockets of tissues (these disintegrate and pieces will end up on the rest of the wash) and loose change, which may damage the machine.

→4

Turn dark items inside out to help preserve their colour and do the same to t-shirts with applied designs. Also make sure you fasten zips and buttons.

5 MIN Wash your whites

Don't be tempted simply to throw whites in the machine. A few minutes spent sorting them properly and dealing with stains means you won't have to soak them for hours to restore their good looks.

BARE ESSENTIALS

stain-removing liquid

washing-up bowl

laundry detergent

washing machine

washing line

→1

Start by sorting the true whites from the pastels. Be ruthless and don't include pale pastels or greys. You should put these in a separate wash for light colours.

→2

Before you launder shirts and blouses, work a stain-removing product into the collar area. Collars often collect grime, especially along the fold.

MONTHLY SCHEDULE

DAILY → Check white items for stains and treat with a suitable stain-removing product as soon as possible.

WEEKLY → Sort through the laundry basket and remove the whites for washing. Then follow steps 1–4 below.

MONTHLY → Tackle greying items, following the tip in the box on the right.

Extra tips

Soak greying whites for 2 hours with the recommended amount of stain-removing detergent and 40 g (1½ oz) borax per litre (2 pints) hot water. Squeeze out, then wash as hot as possible.

Calcium deposits in the water can make your clothes turn grey, so add a capful of water softener to your wash.

→3

→4

Add a capful of laundry detergent to hot water in a bowl and leave the items to soak for 1 hour. Then machine-wash at the hottest recommended temperature.

Dry your whites outside in the sun. Sunlight is a natural whitener so, unless you live in a heavily polluted area, drying your whites outdoors gives best results.

Washing-machine maintenance

10 TIPS

Like other appliances, a washing machine will benefit hugely from a little TLC every few months, especially if you use it frequently. Following these tips doesn't take long and will save you time in the long run as your machine will always work efficiently.

1 AVOID OVERFILLING
Tempting as it is to pile as much as possible into the drum, you must leave room for the water and for the washing to move around. Always follow the manufacturer's recommendations on load sizes. ✓

2 AIR THE DRUM
Make sure you leave the door open after you've used the machine to let the drum air and dry properly. This will prevent mildew. ✓

3 CLEAN THE SEAL
Wipe the rubber door seal regularly with a clean damp cloth. This is where dirty scum builds up and causes an unpleasant smell, especially if you wash at low temperatures and use liquid detergents. ✓

4 CLEAN THE DETERGENT DISPENSER DRAWER
Remove the detergent drawer every few months and wash it in warm water. Don't forget to remove any build-up of soap beneath the drawer. ✓

5 WIPE THE EXTERIOR
Clean the casing regularly using a mild non-abrasive cleaner or gentle washing-up liquid and water on a well wrung-out cloth. Wipe dry with a soft cloth.

6 CLEAN THE FILTER
Depending on the model of your machine and its age, you may need to clean debris regularly from the filter. Consult the manual to see if it's necessary and if it is, how to do it, and how often.

7 RUN A MAINTENANCE WASH
Regularly run an empty maintenance wash using the cottons programme. This is especially important if you mostly wash at low temperatures as it prevents the build-up of soap and limescale deposits in the machine.

8 ADD WASHING SODA OR VINEGAR
When you run a maintenance wash, put a cupful of washing soda or white vinegar in the detergent drawer to help clear any limescale.

9 REMOVE LIMESCALE FROM THE DRAWER
If there's limescale at the back of the detergent drawer, use an old toothbrush soaked in white vinegar to scrub it away. If the deposit is heavy, remove the drawer and soak it in a vinegar-and-water solution.

10 TURN OFF AT THE STOPCOCK
If you're going away on holiday or are leaving the machine unused for a period of time, turn it off at the stopcock. This could prevent a leak in your absence.

Handwash kit

Sometimes handwashing is the only option. You may need something washed quickly, you may not want to put a delicate item in the machine, or hand-washing may be advised on the care label. Whatever the reason, always hand-wash in a dedicated plastic bowl or in the bathroom sink rather than in the kitchen. It's more hygienic that way.

STAIN-REMOVAL BAR
Use on damp fabric to remove stains from items before washing.

STAIN-REMOVAL LIQUID
Like the stain-removal bar (see above), you can use this on damp fabric to remove stains from items before washing. Some also incorporate a brush.

WASHING-UP BOWL
Keep a bowl specially for handwashing. Your normal washing-up bowl may be greasy from food deposits.

NAILBRUSH
Use with detergent to quickly shift grubbiness from shirt collars, cuffs, and under-arm areas.

HANDWASH DETERGENT
Specially formulated to be gentle.

TOWEL
Roll up woollens and other delicate items in a light-coloured towel to remove excess moisture. It cuts down on drying time and protects the fabrics from damage caused by wringing.

RUBBER GLOVES
Wear to protect your hands from the drying effects of detergents.

Handwash clothing

10 MIN

Today's washing machines can cope with most fabrics so if you check your clothing's care labels, you'll probably only need to handwash one or two special items (see opposite). The good news is that with delicate clothes, the less you do, the better the result. Just follow the speedy steps below.

→1

→2

Fill a bowl with warm, not hot, water and add a capful of handwash detergent while the water is running. If colour bleeds when you add the garment, wash it on its own.

Dab any stains with a suitable stain-removing product and gently rub fabric against fabric once or twice to loosen the stain. Rinse and repeat if the stain persists.

Extra tips

Silk garments must be washed by hand. Wash quickly in very cold water with a mild detergent and rinse in cold water too. You can add a little hair conditioner to the final rinse to keep the silk soft and supple.

Wash cashmere quickly by hand in cool water with a very mild detergent. Don't squeeze or wring and rinse in cool water.

Dry flat once you have squeezed out excess water by rolling in a towel.

Handwash vintage clothing made from cotton, linen, and wool mixed with nylon or acrylics. Wash one item at a time in lukewarm water with a mild detergent. Don't wring or scrub, but pat between your palms, allowing the water to run through.

→3

Wash the item by squeezing the soapy water through a couple of times. Never wring or stretch, especially woollens and items with beading, lace, or embroidery.

→4

Rinse in fresh water and repeat until the water is clear. Squeeze out gently in a towel to speed up the drying process, then dry, following the instructions on the care label.

10 TIPS   Indoor drying

Drying washing indoors is a must if you don't have an outdoor line or a tumble dryer. You'll need to be inventive though to ensure that your home doesn't end up damp and/or draped with slow-drying clothes for days on end.

1 CHOOSE THE RIGHT DRYING RACK
Indoor drying racks can hang from the wall or ceiling, or they can be free-standing. Choose one that you can position in a warm but well-ventilated spot and move it into the sunlight if possible. ✔

2 AVOID USING RADIATORS
Don't dry clothes on top of radiators. The clothes will get stiff and may shrink. It also causes condensation and reduces the warmth given out by the radiator. ✔

3 OPEN THE WINDOW
Open a window while you're drying clothes indoors. This prevents condensation, which can lead to damp and mildew. ✔

4 REMOVE EXCESS WATER
Before hanging your clothes to dry, make sure that you've removed all the water you can, otherwise they'll dry slowly and will start to smell damp (see tip 10) ✔

5 **SHAKE WELL**
Before you hang clothes indoors to dry, give each item one short, sharp shake. This helps prevent wrinkles.

6 **ORGANISE THE DRYING RACK**
When arranging clothes on a drying rack, put smaller items, such as knickers and socks, lower down on the rack and leave the upper tiers for larger and longer items like jeans and trousers.

7 **SPACE CLOTHES WELL**
Space clothes out properly on the drying rack so air can circulate around them. This prevents them from drying slowly which will make them smell damp even when they're dry.

8 **USE HANGERS**
Dresses, shirts, and jackets are best dried on hangers to preserve their shape and minimise wrinkles. Start by hanging them in the shower or over the bath while they're dripping, then move them to a drying rack.

9 **DRY WOOL FLAT**
Woollen items need to be dried flat or they'll lose their their shape. Lay them to dry on top of a white or colourfast towel, or use a special mesh rack across the bath.

10 **SPEED UP THE PROCESS**
Don't leave thick jumpers or blankets to dry too slowly or they can start to smell damp. Speed up the process by directing an electric fan towards the clothes but not too close, and never leave unattended.

10 TIPS Using a tumble dryer

A tumble dryer gives you dry clothes at the touch of a button you don't have to depend on the vagaries of the weather. It will also increase your energy bills and wear out your clothes faster so only tumble-dry when you need dry clothes fast.

1 DO CHECK THE CARE LABELS
Most clothes can go in the dryer, except for heat-sensitive fabrics such as Lycra®, certain woollens, and very delicate silks. Some fabrics need a cool setting. ✓

2 SQUEEZE OUT WET ITEMS
Extract as much water as possible from your wash before you put it in the tumble dryer. This will save you time and money. ✓

3 DO SHAKE OUT AS YOU LOAD
As you put items in the tumble dryer, shake them out first, one at a time. This helps remove creases that would otherwise be set by the heat. ✓

4 AVOID OVERFILLING
Don't overfill the drum. If you do, your clothes will emerge with more creases. Check the manual for the recommended (dry) weight of fabric per load and per programme. ✓

5 AVOID OVERDRYING

Items that have been tumble-dried for too long will become wrinkly. If this happens, add a wet bath towel to the dryer and run it again. This is an effective but energy-greedy remedy.

6 DO CHECK FOR SMALL ITEMS

When you remove the dry load, turn the drum with your hand to check that small items such as handkerchiefs and underwear aren't still inside.

7 KEEP CHILDREN SAFE

Never allow children to play or interfere with the tumble dryer and keep them well away while it's in use.

8 CLEAN THE FILTER

Remove fluff from the filter (usually on the front edge of the drum) after every drying cycle or there's a risk of fire. Regularly wipe around the filter opening too, as fluff can gather there.

9 SWITCH OFF BETWEEN USES

When the dryer's not in use, switch it off, unplug it at the wall, and make sure the door's closed. This protects from the risk of an electrical fire and stops children from tampering with the dryer (see tip 7).

10 CLEAN INSIDE AND OUT

Every few months, wipe the inside of the dryer with a cloth that's been barely dampened with warm, soapy water. Occasionally wipe the exterior with a damp cloth too.

Ironing kit

Before you tackle a pile of wrinkled shirts, make sure you have the right equipment. That means not only a clean iron and a board that's no higher than hip-level, but also a ready supply of hangers and a pressing cloth for use on suits and delicate fabrics. A lavender-and-water spray is a useful addition.

WATER SPRAY
Fill with tap water and use to dampen over-dry items before ironing.

LAVENDER OIL
A few drops added to the water spray will make your clothes smell fresh.

IRONING BOARD COVER
Make sure you buy a well-padded, heat-resistant cover that's the correct size for your ironing board.

SOLEPLATE CLEANING WIPES
Used regularly, these ensure your iron runs smoothly over the fabric.

COTTON PRESSING CLOTHS
Use a thin pressing cloth between the iron and the fabric to prevent suit material going shiny.

DESCALING SOLUTION
Use every 6 months or so to get rid of mineral deposits in your iron's water tank.

STEAM IRON
Choose an iron with a large-capacity water tank so you don't have to waste time refilling it. An automatic shut-off function will prevent you from scorching your clothes.

IRONING BOARD
The bigger your ironing board, the faster you'll be able to iron as you won't need to move the clothes around so often. Always buy a height-adjustable board.

SELECTION OF HANGERS
Hang clothes straight after ironing to stop them wrinkling. Hang delicate clothes on padded hangers and use unpadded hangers for other clothes.

139

10 TIPS Speed ironing

Certain shirts and blouses have to be ironed but items like towels and underwear don't. Use these simple tips and techniques to keep your ironing to the absolute minimum and to speed up the ironing that you really can't avoid.

1 USE FABRIC CONDITIONER
Add some fabric conditioner to the final rinse of your wash and your clothes will emerge from the machine with fewer wrinkles. ✔

2 TAKE ADVANTAGE OF THE TUMBLE DRYER
Used properly (see pp.136–7), the tumble dryer will save you ironing many items. For best results, take clothes out before they're completely dry, then shake them out straight away. ✔

3 FOLD BEFORE IRONING
Whether they are line-dried or tumble-dried, instead of dumping your clothes in a pile while you get around to ironing them, fold them carefully. You'll then have fewer creases to contend with. ✔

4 BUY "WRINKLE-RESISTANT"
Man-made fibres are often labelled "wrinkle resistant". These fabrics won't need ironing but it's worth hanging items made from them in the bathroom where the steam will remove any creases. ✔

5 KEEP IRONING TO A MINIMUM
Hang skirts and dresses to dry so you don't have to iron them, and don't bother to iron towels, underwear, or bedding.

6 IRON AT THE CORRECT TEMPERATURE
Check the care label instructions before ironing. If you set the iron to the correct temperature, you'll iron faster and you'll avoid damaging the clothes.

7 IRON FROM COOLEST TO HOTTEST
Start by ironing the clothes that need the coolest temperature and work your way up to those that need the hottest. That way you won't have to wait for the iron to cool down.

8 IRON COTTON AND LINEN
To look their best, cotton and linen clothing should always be ironed. For best results, iron while slightly damp, or dampen a little with the spray on your steam iron or with a hand-held water spray.

9 IRON TEA TOWELS AND HANDKERCHIEFS
If at all possible, you should iron tea towels and handkerchiefs, if only because it helps to sterilize them.

10 AVOID IRONING DIRTY CLOTHES
Never be tempted to try and freshen up grubby clothes by giving them a quick iron. The heat from the iron can set any stains in the fabric and they'll be impossible to remove.

3 MIN Iron a collar and cuffs

There are always emergencies when, no matter how hard you try, you just can't find time to iron the shirt or blouse you need in a hurry. The only thing to do is cheat. Three minutes are all it takes to set the iron and ironing board up and iron the collar and cuffs. Keep your jacket on and no one will ever know!

→1

→2

Lay the collar flat on the ironing board and iron the inside. Then fold the collar along the natural fold line and iron the outside, particularly along the fold.

Slip one shoulder over the narrow end of the ironing board. Iron the shoulder panel towards the sleeve, then turn the shirt round and iron the other panel.

BEFORE YOU BEGIN

ADJUST THE IRONING BOARD → Make sure the board's at hip height.

ADJUST THE TEMPERATURE → Make sure the temperature's correctly set to match the fabric you're ironing and give the iron time to reach that temperature.

HAVE EVERYTHING TO HAND → You may need a water spray to get rid of firm creases.

Extra tips

It's quicker to iron shirts when they're still a little damp. If they're too dry, dampen by spraying with the spray on your iron or with a hand-held spray.

To iron gathers, place the iron with the gathers opening in the direction of the tip of the iron, then wiggle the tip into each gather in turn.

→3

→4

Make sure the cuffs are unbuttoned then place one cuff on the ironing board, buttons facing down, and iron the inside using the tip of the iron.

Turn the cuff over and iron the outside. Avoid ironing any part of the sleeve and don't iron over the buttons in case they melt. Repeat for the other cuff.

Iron a shirt front and sleeves

3 MIN

There's no doubt that a shirt looks smarter when it's ironed, even a shirt that's made from non-iron fabric. If you've already ironed the collar and cuffs (see pp.142–3), you only need another 3 minutes to iron the front and sleeves. With practice, you can iron the whole shirt in 5 minutes.

→1

Slip the shirt front, buttons facing upwards, over the ironing board. Iron in between the buttons then iron the rest of the front. Iron the other shirt front.

→2

Slip the back of the shirt over the ironing board and iron it. Revolve the shirt, smoothing it out with your hands and ironing it until you reach the other front.

Extra tips

To iron silk garments, leave them slightly damp, turn them inside out, and use the coolest setting. Don't spray any areas with water as this will leave a mark.

To iron a sequined garment, put it face down on a thick towel, lay a pressing cloth on top and iron over that on a cool setting.

To iron lined clothes, turn inside out to iron the lining first, then turn the right way and iron the outer fabric.

Always iron vintage clothing with care, especially if there's no care label. Hot ironing isn't a good idea. It's better to use the coolest setting and/or a pressing cloth to protect the fabric. Press, don't drag.

→3

Lay the sleeve along the board so its side seams are lying flat. Iron along the sleeve, moving from cuff to shoulder. Repeat for the other sleeve.

→4

Don't ruin your good work by letting the shirt gather creases. Place it on a hanger and fasten the top few buttons to help the shirt keep its shape.

Fold a shirt

There's nothing more annoying than wasting time trying to find a particular shirt, blouse, jumper, or t-shirt. Master this speedy folding technique, then you can stow your tops in a neat stack on a shelf or in a drawer. When it's time to get dressed, it only takes a moment to find the top you need.

With the shirt on a flat surface, button it up at the top, middle, and bottom buttons. This helps the shirt keep its shape. Don't bother to button the cuffs.

Now lay the shirt face down. Leaving the sleeves hanging at either side, fold each side of the shirt inwards so that they meet down the middle of the back.

Extra tips

If the shirt has a shirt-tail, fold it up between steps 3 and 4 to make a straight line before you fold the rest of the shirt into thirds.

To fold tailored trousers ready to hang, lay one leg on top of the other and align the front and back creases. Hang by the bottom edge or fold over a trouser hanger.

For wrinkle-free packing of suits and dresses, hang in garment bags then fold the bags into your case.

To get rid of wrinkles from clothes that have been in a suitcase, unpack as soon as you arrive and hang the garments on a plastic hanger in the bathroom while you have a shower.

→3

→4

Pick up one sleeve and lay it down the back so it's aligned with the side fold. Repeat with the other sleeve. Your shirt should now be in the shape of a rectangle.

Fold up the bottom third, including the sleeves and cuffs. Then fold the top third, including the collar, back over the other two thirds.

10 TIPS Bedlinen care

Although duvets, pillows, and blankets need cleaning, the good news is that you don't have to do it more than once or twice a year – and in between you can easily keep them fresh. If in doubt about how to clean, follow the advice on the care label.

1 SPOT-TREAT STAINS
Deal with stains on pillows, blankets, and duvets as soon as you notice them. Use handwash laundry detergent and a damp sponge, rinse, then dry in a warm place or dry with a hairdryer.

2 FRESHEN UP PILLOWS
Every month, freshen pillows by putting them in a hot tumble dryer for 15 minutes (the heat kills dust mites) or by hanging them outside.

3 WASH PILLOWS
Every 6 months, machine-wash pillows on the gentlest cycle, unless the care label states they're not washable. Don't add fabric conditioner. Finish either by tumble- or line-drying.

4 FRESHEN DUVETS
Every 6 months, freshen duvets by tumble-drying on a hot setting. If the care label states they can't be tumble-dried, hang outdoors for a few hours.

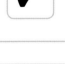

5 WASH DUVETS INFREQUENTLY

Duvets only need to be washed once a year, and less frequently if they contain feathers. Only machine-wash if advised on the care label.

6 LAUNDERETTE-WASH LARGE DUVETS

Kingsize and super kingsize duvets won't fit in a domestic washing machine or tumble dryer. You'll need to take them to the launderette.

7 PREVENT CLUMPING IN THE DRYER

To prevent the filling in a duvet or in pillows from clumping together when tumble-dried, always pop a couple of colourfast tennis balls in the dryer with the items.

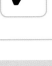

8 REVIVE GREYING SHEETS

To brighten greying bedlinen, soak for 2 hours with stain-removing detergent and 40 g (1½ oz) per litre (2 pints) hot water before putting it in the wash.

9 RESHAPE WHILE DAMP

If you have a machine-washable blanket, measure it before washing so you can reshape it to its original dimensions while it's drying.

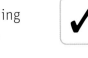

10 DRY-CLEAN WOOLLEN BLANKETS

Many woollen bedspreads and blankets have to be dry cleaned (check the care label) although you can spot-treat stains in the same way as other bedding (see tip 1).

10 TIPS Successful dry-cleaning

It may be expensive, but dry-cleaning is the only way to keep some of the finest, most delicate garments in your wardrobe looking their best. If the item's precious, consider going to a specialist rather than using an express service.

1 AVOID BUYING TOO MANY DRY-CLEAN ITEMS
To reduce the inconvenience as well as your dry-cleaning bills, avoid buying clothes that are dry-clean-only. Before you buy anything new, make a habit of checking the care label first.

2 CHECK GARMENT LABELS CAREFULLY
Ignore the garment's care label at your peril. The most likely reason for recommending that an item be dry-cleaned is to avoid it shrinking, going out of shape, or leaking dye into the wash.

3 LOOK FOR THE LETTER "P"
If an item has a care label with an letter P or F, in a circle this means that it must be dry-cleaned specially carefully. Point this out in case your dry cleaner isn't prepared to accept responsibility.

4 KEEP MATCHING ITEMS TOGETHER
Dry-clean sets of items at the same time, in case the colours fade. For example, send suit jackets and trousers or pairs of curtains to the dry cleaners together

5 KNOW YOUR RIGHTS

Care labels are covered by consumer law in most countries so if a dry-clean-only item has shrunk when you get it back from the cleaners, you can ask the manufacturer to repair or replace it.

6 AVOID STORING IN PLASTIC BAGS

When you get your clothes home, remove the plastic cover as it can stain the clothes indelibly. Replace the wire hanger with a plastic, wooden, or padded one, too. A good hanger will extend the life of your clothes.

7 GET RID OF THE SMELL

If there's a smell of dry-cleaning solvent on your clothes when you get them back, don't hang them in your wardrobe straight away. First let them air outside or in a well-ventilated room for a day.

8 AVOID LEAVING STAINED ITEMS TOO LONG

If you have a stained dry-clean-only item, don't leave it lying around for days. Take it to the dry cleaners as soon as possible, point out the stain, and say what caused it. This will help them treat it correctly.

9 AVOID WASHING DRY-CLEAN-ONLY ITEMS REPEATEDLY

If you do decide to go ahead and wash a dry-clean-only item, don't do it often. The impact of washing may only become apparent after several washes.

10 AVOID DRY-CLEANING FEATHERS AND DOWN

Dry-cleaning strips the natural oils from down and feathers in pillows and coats, and it's this that keeps you warm. Laundering at a low temperature is often best, but consult the care label first.

Shoe-cleaning kit

You can polish your shoes the old-fashioned way by removing surface dirt, applying wax with a shoe brush, rubbing it off with a second brush, and buffing to a shine with a duster. This only takes a few minutes but if you prefer, you can use an even faster self-shining product. Specialist products include cleaners for suede and nubuck, as well as waterproofing sprays.

KITCHEN TOWEL
Use to apply baby oil and also to pack into wet shoes to absorb the moisture.

SHOE BRUSHES
Use one to apply polish and another for rubbing the polish off. Keep a pair for each colour.

DUSTERS
Use to buff shoes to a shine. Keep one for each colour polish.

BICARBONATE OF SODA
Sprinkle in shoes to remove odour overnight.

BABY OIL
Use a spot on a sheet of kitchen towel to restore the shine to patent leather.

WATERPROOFING SPRAY
Use on new shoes before you wear them and reapply to clean shoes from time to time.

SUEDE CLEANER
Specially formulated for suede and nubuck, these cleaners often incorporate a plastic brush in the cap.

MICROFIBRE CLOTH
This works just as well as a duster to buff shoes and is less likely to leave fluff behind.

SELF-SHINING POLISH
Just a wipe makes shoes look like new, but it doesn't feed the leather like traditional polish.

RUBBER GLOVES
To protect your hands when cleaning shoes.

TRADITIONAL SHOE POLISH
Use to nourish the leather and stop it drying out and cracking.

NEWSPAPER
In the interests of hygiene, use some newspaper to protect surfaces when you're cleaning shoes.

Removing stains

Stain-removal kit

The secret to successful stain removal is to act quickly and to blot up spills with kitchen towel as soon as they happen. Always work from the outside edge of the stain towards the centre and dab, don't scrub. For tough stains, start with the mildest remedy and work up to the knockout chemical attack.

CARPET-CLEANING SPRAY
Use to remove red wine and urine stains from carpets.

METHYLATED SPIRITS
Use for removing tough grass stains and felt-tip pen marks.

TALCUM POWDER
Useful for removing greasy stains.

DETERGENT WITH OXYGEN BLEACH
Containing hydrogen peroxide (see opposite), it is gentler than household bleach and suits many fabrics.

CLEAN WHITE CLOTHS
Use to absorb stains. Avoid coloured cloths in case the dye transfers to the item you're cleaning.

WASHING-UP BOWL
Put clothes in to soak.

STAIN-REMOVAL BAR
Use before you wash for dealing with stains on clothes. See also p.130.

STAIN-REMOVAL LIQUID
Keep this in your armoury of spot-cleaning products. See also p.130.

KITCHEN TOWEL
Use this as quickly as possible to blot up spills and so avoid stains.

SODA WATER
Encourages spills like red wine and urine to bubble to the surface so you can blot them up.

SPONGE
Use to dab at stains, working from the outside in.

RUBBER GLOVES
To protect your hands while you're working with stain removers.

HYDROGEN PEROXIDE
A last resort for removing otherwise unshiftable old sweat stains.

BRANDED STAIN REMOVERS
Keep a selection in your kit to remove specific types of stain.

5 MIN

Remove a red wine stain from a carpet

Red wine, unlike white, is renowned for staining. But act swiftly and you won't have a problem. The sooner you splash on some soda water, the greater your chances of getting rid of the stain completely.

BARE ESSENTIALS

kitchen towel

soda water

sponges

aerosol carpet cleaner

vacuum cleaner

Use kitchen towel to absorb as much wine as possible. Blot from the outside of the stain towards the centre to prevent the stain from spreading.

Splash a little soda water onto the stain to encourage the wine to bubble up to the surface. Then blot it with a sponge, taking care not to rub. Repeat if necessary.

BEFORE YOU BEGIN

PUT ON RUBBER GLOVES → These will protect your hands from the carpet cleaner, which may contain toxic ingredients.

CLEAR THE AREA → Move furniture and make sure rugs are folded out of the way.

KEEP PETS AND CHILDREN AWAY → They must not come into contact with the carpet cleaner as it may contain toxic ingredients.

Extra tips

Don't believe the one about covering a red-wine stain with salt. It simply sets the stain.

To remove red wine from clothing and upholstery, sponge with lukewarm water, blot to remove excess, then use a proprietary stain remover designed for wine and fruit-juice stains.

→3

Thoroughly shake the can of aerosol carpet cleaner, then spray it onto the affected area. Work the foam in gently using a clean damp sponge.

→4

Leave until the carpet is completely dry, then vacuum the affected area. If the stain remains, repeat the process, this time starting from step 3.

Remove ink stains from a sofa

3 MIN

Don't panic if you discover your favourite sofa has been used as a drawing board. Many inks today are washable and will come out easily. This simple method works for both felt-tip and ballpoint inks.

BARE ESSENTIALS

kitchen towel

upholstery cleaning spray

sponge

colourfast towel

→1

→2

As soon as you can, blot the stained area with a piece of kitchen towel to remove any excess ink. Blot from the outside to the inside to avoid spreading the stain further.

Following the manufacturer's instructions, spray a little upholstery cleaner on the stain, then leave the product to work for the recommended time.

Extra tips

Remove ink stains from washable clothing by using an oxygen-bleach detergent, a branded stain remover for ink stains (follow the manufacturer's instructions), or by dabbing with methylated spirit (test first for colourfastness on an inconspicuous part of the garment), followed by rinsing and washing.

Remove ballpoint ink from clothing by using a solvent such as dry-cleaning fluid, lighter fuel, or methylated spirit, or by dabbing with surgical spirit or vodka. Test first for colourfastness. After use, rinse in cold water, then wash as normal.

Don't wash ink-stained clothing until you have removed as much stain as you can or the stain will set.

→3

Blot the area with a clean damp sponge, being careful not to spread the stain. If the stain remains, reapply the upholstery cleaner and leave to work as before.

→4

Finish by removing excess moisture from the area. Place an old, colourfast towel on top to absorb the moisture and leave until the area's almost dry, then leave to air-dry.

Remove grass stains from clothing

5 MIN

Light grass stains may come out in the wash without a pre-wash soaking but to be sure, you'll need to use a stain-removing product, especially if the clothing is white or light-coloured.

BARE ESSENTIALS

knife

washing-up bowl

stain-removing stick

→1

→2

Working as quickly as possible, start by scraping away any loose bits of grass from the surface of the fabric using a blunt knife. Go carefully to avoid damaging the fabric.

Immerse the stained area in a bowl filled with cold water. Leave to soak for a few minutes, then rub fabric against fabric to break up the stain.

ACTION PLAN

BEFORE YOU START → Put on rubber gloves to protect your hands from drying out.

AS YOU WORK → Make sure you soak the clothing in cold water as grass is a protein and hot water will set the stain.

AFTERWARDS → Follow the correct washing and drying instructions for the fabric.

Extra tips

To remove old grass stains, dab with a 1:4 solution of methylated spirit and water, rinse in warm soapy water, then launder or dry clean.

To remove grass stains from delicates, apply the stain remover using a cloth with a gentle circular movement, then hand wash.

Apply a stain-removing stick and again rub fabric against fabric. If the stain still persists, rinse, apply more stain remover, and rub again.

Finish by rinsing in plenty of clean water, then launder the item at the highest possible temperature recommended on the care label.

Remove grease stains from clothing

5 MIN

Tackling grease stains requires a fast two-pronged attack. First remove excess grease by dry-blotting and then move onto using water and detergent. If the stain's old, take the garment to the dry cleaner.

BARE ESSENTIALS

kitchen towel

sponge

hand-wash laundry detergent

washing-up bowl

→1

→2

As soon as you can, lay the stained area on a piece of kitchen towel to help absorb the grease. Blot the other side of the fabric with another piece of kitchen towel.

Repeat using clean pieces of kitchen towel until the worst of the grease has been absorbed, then dampen the area using a sponge and cold water.

Extra tips

Removing grease from upholstery, requires a similar approach to removing it from clothing. Blot up as much grease as possible using kitchen towel, then sprinkle with talcum powder, Fuller's earth, or cornflour. Leave to absorb the grease, then vacuum off using the dusting-brush attachment. If the stain persists, follow steps 3–4 on p.173.

Remove grease from a carpet by blotting with a piece of kitchen towel, then using dry-cleaning fluid. Or use a dry-stick spot cleaner to absorb the grease, leave for a few minutes, then brush or vacuum away.

Remove grease from wallpaper using dry-cleaning fluid. Test for colourfastness on an inconspicuous part of the paper first.

→3

Put a little hand-wash laundry detergent on the stain and work it in. Don't rub or the stain might spread. Soak at the highest temperature recommended for the fabric.

→4

Soak for 30 minutes. If the stain persists, add some hand-wash detergent and soak again. Finally wash at the highest possible temperature or handwash if required.

Remove perspiration marks from clothing

3 MIN

Don't leave sweaty clothes sitting in the laundry basket or the stains will be more difficult to remove. Today's oxygen-bleach detergents work well on a wide range of fabrics and speed up stain-removal.

BARE ESSENTIALS

oxygen-bleach detergent

washing-up bowl

→1

→2

Take the item of clothing off as soon as possible. Fill a washing-up bowl with warm water, add the clothing, and leave it to soak for 10 minutes. This loosens the stain.

Remove the clothing, refill the bowl with clean warm water, and add the recommended amount of oxygen-bleach detergent.

Extra tips

If you notice unsightly white deodorant marks on your clothes, there's no need to change. Try rubbing the area with a pair of tights or with a dark sock.

To remove perspiration stains the traditional way, sponge with a solution of 15ml (1tbsp) white vinegar to 250ml (½ pint) warm water, then rinse and wash as normal. If the garment can't be washed, sponge with the vinegar solution (test first for colourfastness), then dry clean.

To remove old perspiration stains from washable fabric, soften the stain first by dabbing with a little glycerin. Alternatively, if the fabric is white, pour a little hydrogen peroxide on the stained area, rub it in gently, leave for 5 minutes, then wash as normal.

Dissolve the oxygen-bleach detergent completely, then immerse the clothing in the solution. Gently rub fabric against fabric in the area of the stain.

Leave to soak for a further 30 minutes, then rinse in cold water. Once the stain has gone, launder at the hottest temperature recommended on the care label.

Remove urine stains from a carpet

10 MIN

Urine can remove dye and may damage wool and nylon, so eliminate it from carpets and fabrics as quickly as you can. The smell of cat urine lingers too, so use a deodorising spray after step 4.

BARE ESSENTIALS

kitchen towel

soda water, sponges

carpet-cleaning spray

spray bottle filled with water

towel

→1

Blot up the urine as soon as possible using kitchen towel. Use fresh pieces of towel and keep blotting until the towel comes away dry.

→2

Pour a little soda water onto the stain to bring the urine to the surface, then soak up the moisture with a dry sponge or with more kitchen towel.

ACTION PLAN

BEFORE YOU START → Put on rubber gloves for hygiene reasons.

CLEAR THE AREA → Move furniture and make sure rugs are folded out of the way.

AFTERWARDS → If you need to speed up the drying process, you can use a hairdryer on a cool setting after step 4.

Extra tips

To remove dried-on urine, dampen the stain with a sponge, then continue from step 2.

To remove urine from clothes, soak overnight in warm water with a little biological detergent, then wash and dry in the usual way.

→3

Spray the stained area with a carpet-cleaning product, then work the product gently into the stain from the outside in, using a damp sponge.

→4

Using a clean sponge and a spray bottle of water, rinse the area. Take care not to get the carpet too wet. Finish by using an old towel to soak up any moisture.

Remove blood stains from clothing

5 MIN

As with all stains, the longer blood sits on a fabric, the tougher it is to remove. These instructions work for stains a day old or less. If they're older, you may need to repeat steps 2–4. And because blood's a protein, only use cold water on it or the stain will set hard.

→1

Remove the item of clothing as soon as possible and immerse it in a washing-up bowl filled with cold water. This will help to loosen the blood.

→2

Rub a little handwash laundry detergent into the remaining stain. Rub the area firmly between your fists, with your palms facing each other.

ACTION PLAN

BEFORE YOU START → If the blood is fresh, rinse the clothing under a cold tap to flush away excess blood before starting step 1.

AS YOU WORK → Be sure to soak the clothing in cold water as hot water will set the stain.

AFTERWARDS → Make sure the stain has been removed before ironing, or the heat of the iron will set the stain.

Extra tips

To remove blood stains from delicates, apply the handwash laundry detergent with a sponge, using a gentle circular movement. Rinse then dry.

To remove blood stains from upholstery, blot with kitchen towel, dab with water and a little handwash laundry detergent, spray with water, then blot dry.

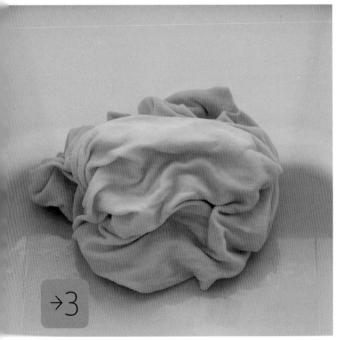

→3

Leave the wet clothing for 15 minutes for the detergent to work. If you're treating several garments, be careful not to let the damp articles touch or the colours may run.

→4

If the stain's gone completely, rinse thoroughly and hang to dry. If there's still some residual stain, wash the item according to the care label.

Remove food stains from upholstery

4 MIN

Stains from food are common on upholstery but can usually be removed in a matter of minutes. Follow the simple steps below to remove non-liquid stains such as jam or chocolate.

BARE ESSENTIALS

knife, kitchen towel, plastic bowl

hand-wash laundry detergent, sponges

upholstery cleaning spray

spray bottle filled with water colourfast towel

→1

→2

Start by scraping off any excess food using the blunt edge of a knife. Take care not to spread the food, so be sure to wipe the knife clean on kitchen towel as you work.

Follow the manufacturer's instructions to make a solution of hand-wash laundry detergent and cool water. Sponge on gently without rubbing to avoid spreading the stain.

Extra tips

To remove black or white coffee stains from upholstery, blot the excess liquid using a piece of kitchen towel, then pour on a little soda water and blot with a clean piece of kitchen towel. Repeat until the stain has gone or, if you can't remove it all by this method, continue with steps 3–4 below.

To remove a tea stain from upholstery, blot the stain to remove the excess tea using a piece of kitchen towel, then spray on some cold water and blot with a clean piece of kitchen towel. If this doesn't work, try dabbing with a solution of biological detergent and water, then rinse this out with a spray of cold water. Blot dry with a colourfast towel, then leave to air-dry.

→3

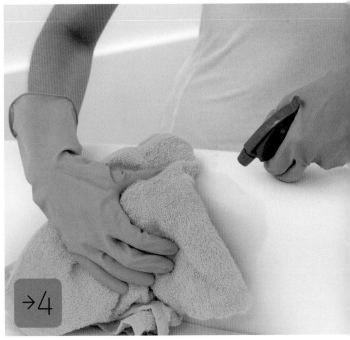

→4

If the stain persists, spray a little upholstery cleaner on the stain. Blot with a clean damp sponge, being careful not to spread the stain.

Using a spray filled with tap water, moisten – don't soak – the stained area, then blot it with a colourfast towel. When it's almost dry, leave to air-dry.

Coping with
children and pets

10 TIPS Successful delegation

Family housework doesn't have to be done just by one person. You need help, especially if you do a paid job too. Encourage everyone in the house to feel part of the cleaning team and if you find you're still struggling, it may be time to employ a cleaner.

1 START THEM YOUNG
Even toddlers can start to help their parents by putting away their toys, placing dirty clothes in a laundry basket, and carrying things to and from the table.

2 SAY WHAT YOU EXPECT
Once children are 10 or more, you can expect them to make their own beds, sort their dirty laundry, vacuum their room, help with washing up, and load and empty the dishwasher.

3 GET CHILDREN'S HELP AT MEALTIMES
If children are hanging around waiting for a meal, involve them in preparations by asking them to clear and set the table. Make sure they make an effort to put their own dishes away too.

4 GIVE CHILDREN CHOICES
To encourage children to help with chores, give them a choice. Ask if they'd like to empty the dishwasher or tidy the coffee table. They'll be happier to carry out a task if it's one they've chosen themselves.

5 GIVE PARTNERS CHOICES
Giving a choice can also work with partners. Explain what needs doing around the house one evening and ask your partner which of the tasks they'd like to do.

6 PRAISE GENEROUSLY
Even if the job isn't done as well as you might do it, don't criticize. You can point out what needs to be done to complete the job, but remember to praise what has been done.

7 EXPLAIN WHY
Children will be more likely to help if they understand the purpose of tidying. Explain that it will give them more space to play, make things easier to find, and prevent their toys getting stepped on and broken.

8 AVOID SUPERVISING OLDER CHILDREN
Avoid supervising older children when they're cleaning. Let them take responsibility for a task and they'll feel more satisfied when it's completed.

9 HELP THE CLEANER ON THE FIRST DAY
The first day your cleaner comes, make sure you're there to oversee things. Have a list of jobs you'd like to have done so you can help your cleaner to establish a routine.

10 TELL THE CLEANER WHAT TO USE
Point out the materials you'd like your cleaner to use, or you may find bleach used everywhere or bathroom sponges being used for washing the dishes.

Child's bedroom speed-clean

15 MIN

Although children can help around the house from a young age, when it comes to transforming their bedrooms from chaos to calm sanctuary, chances are you'll have to take the lead. In 15 minutes, you should be able carry out this speedy clean.

1 BRING IN THE FRESH AIR
Open the window to let in some fresh air while you clean. It will also reduce humidity and warmth, which will help prevent dust mites.

2 MAKE THE BED
Shake out the bedding and leave it to air while you do the rest of the jobs. Before you leave the room, make up the bed, plumping the pillows and smoothing out the duvet.

3 CLEAR UP MESSY THINGS
If your child has been painting, colouring, or doing other messy activities, put everything away. If the child's around, get him or her to lend a hand to encourage them to help in future.

4 CHECK FOR STAINS
Check the carpet and upholstery for spills or stains. Deal immediately with any that you find, using the appropriate detergent and stain-removal method.

5 TIDY UP CLOTHES

Pick up any clothes from the floor and give them a firm shake to remove dust and dirt. Then hang them in the wardrobe or fold them and put them away in drawers.

6 CHECK FOR DIRTY CLOTHES

Ideally your child will have a laundry basket in the room, so if you come across dirty clothes pop them in. Alternatively, make a pile near the door to take to the laundry bin when you leave the room.

7 DEAL WITH TOYS

Pick up toys and replace in toy-storage containers. If you come across any that are grubby, give them a wipe with a damp sponge. If they can be machine-washed, add them to the laundry pile.

8 DAMP-DUST

Using a damp microfibre cloth, quickly wipe bedside tables and other surfaces to remove dust. If lampshades are dusty, make sure they're unplugged then wipe them with a barely damp cloth.

9 EMPTY THE WASTE BIN

Empty the waste bin, separating any items that can be recycled and putting the rest with the household rubbish. Line with a clean liner.

10 FINISH BY VACUUMING

Focus on the most-used areas like the doorway and alongside the bed. Use the crevice nozzle in the corners. If there's time, pull out the bed and vacuum behind.

Child's room storage

Toys, books, clothes, crayons, notebooks, and teddies – you'll find all this and more in a child's bedroom. Clever and attractive storage is the key to keeping it all tidy. Choose multi-purpose items wherever possible, make use of the end of the bed, under the bed, and of shelves, and store everything where the child can reach it. And of course, as soon as she's old enough, encourage her to keep her own room tidy.

TOY TIDY
Toys your child might want while she's in bed can be stored in a toy tidy that buttons over the side of the bed.

TOY TRUNK
Keep toys that are used less often or spare bedding in a decorative toy trunk.

UNDERBED STORAGE
Use baskets or fabric organisers to store small, often-used toys under the bed. This is the ideal location for small children's toys as they can easily reach their playthings. In an older child's room, choose boxes with lids for longer-term storage.

PENCIL HOLDER
Pop pens and pencils in a pretty plastic cup to keep them all in one place instead of scattered around the room.

BOOKCASE
Choose a bookcase with cubbyholes or a modular unit if you want to store a variety of items instead of just books.

MAGAZINE FILE
Use to store magazines and comics and keep them all in one place. There are plenty of decorative versions around that don't immediately shout "office".

SOFT TOYS
Get your child to put her soft toys "to bed" in their storage basket. It will encourage her to go to bed too. And make sure that all soft toys can be washed easily.

BOX FILES
Encourage older children to file their homework in decorative box files, that way it will stay clean and free of creases.

CUSHION
Use a cushion on top of a trunk to provide extra seating.

STORAGE BASKETS
Have a variety of sizes and label them – with a picture of the contents if you like, to encourage your child to tidy her things away.

Remove pet hair from upholstery

3 MIN

Pet hair on soft furnishings not only looks unsightly, but it also provides food for dust mites. Remove pet hair daily – especially if there are people with allergies in the home – using this quick and easy technique.

BARE ESSENTIALS

rubber glove

vacuum cleaner

dusting-brush attachment

→1

Put on a rubber glove then dampen it (and ensure it is free of detergent) by holding your gloved hand under cold, running water.

→2

With your damp, gloved hand, palm facing down, use a firm brushing motion to gently rub the upholstery. Focus on the areas with the pet hair.

Extra tips

The best way to remove pet hair from a carpet, is to vacuum it. If there are any particularly densely covered areas, pick up the worst of the hair using a damp rubber glove, as below, then vacuum. Clumps of animal hair can block a vacuum cleaner.

Your first line of attack against dust mites and dander (tiny particles of an animal's dried hair or skin that dust mites thrive on) is your vacuum cleaner. Use it regularly around the home and make sure it has a HEPA filter (see pp.21 and 186).

Your second line of attack is to groom your pets regularly and do all you can to prevent them from developing dry, flaky skin (see p.187).

→3

Scoop up the small ball of hair that will have stuck to the damp glove, and throw it away. You may need to rinse and dampen the rubber glove again and repeat.

→4

Vacuum the upholstery using the dusting-brush attachment to pick up any remaining hair. Ideally, use a vacuum cleaner with a HEPA filter (see pp.21 and 186).

Pet-zone kit

However much we love our fluffy companions, there's no doubt they create extra work. As well as scattering hair everywhere, pets also carry bacteria that can be dangerous to humans. Be sure you've got the right kit for caring for and cleaning up after your pets, and clean up as quickly as you can. You must also tackle your general household cleaning extra thoroughly.

PET BLANKET
If your cat or dog likes a certain chair, use a machine-washable blanket to cover it.

PET BASKET
Choose a design that's easy to clean.

PET BRUSH
Use to groom your cat or dog, but regularly clean the hair from the bristles.

MACHINE-WASHABLE PET BOWLS
Choose dishwasher-safe pet bowls and wash them regularly.

SPONGE
Keep a dedicated "pet" sponge and only use for pet-related cleaning jobs.

ANTI-BACTERIAL WIPES
Use for wiping up accidents around the house as well as wiping baskets and pet accessories such as brushes.

PET DUVETS
Choose one that's machine-washable.

DISINFECTANT SPRAY
Use to clean around your pet's feeding area.

LIDS FOR PET FOOD
Use to avoid the smell from open cans of food permeating the fridge.

COMPOSTABLE BAGS
Use to collect pet waste. Don't put in the kitchen bin. Either flush the contents down the toilet or put the sealed bag in the dustbin.

RUBBER GLOVES
Reserve a pair of rubber gloves for cleaning up after your pet.

10 TIPS Dealing with allergies

For anyone with allergies, the main aim of housework should be to reduce dust and get rid of dust mites. Most importantly, vacuum regularly, choose the right flooring, and keep your pets out of the bedroom.

1 GET THE RIGHT VACUUM CLEANER
Make sure you have a vacuum cleaner with a HEPA (high-efficiency particulate air) filter. Dust and vacuum the house at least once a week, prioritising the rooms you spend most time in.

2 CHOOSE SOFT FURNISHINGS WITH CARE
Dust mites, pet hair, and dander cling to carpets, so opt for bare floors with washable rugs. Curtains also attract dust mites, so vacuum and wash them regularly. Leather sofas are better than fabric ones.

3 BUY ALLERGEN-PROOF BEDDING COVERS
Buy allergen-proof covers for pillows, mattresses, and duvets. These are tightly woven to seal out allergens from your bedding, but they're still soft and comfortable to sleep on.

4 WASH BEDDING AT A HIGH TEMPERATURE
Wash sheets, pillowcases, mattress covers, and blankets at 60°C (140°F) to kill dust mites. If the care label recommends a cool wash, placing items in the freezer for 6 hours will also kill them.

5 KEEP THINGS COOL AND DRY

Dust mites love warmth and moisture, so open windows, keep the temperature down, and use a dehumidifier if necessary. This is particularly important in the bedroom, where mites and allergens thrive.

6 CHOOSE PET BEDDING WITH CARE

Choose pet bedding that can be machine-washed and wash it at least every two weeks. Choose wipe-clean plastic pet baskets.

7 BATH PETS REGULARLY

Although cats hate it, regular bathing reduces the amount of allergens that are spread around the home. If you start a monthly bath routine when a cat or dog is a small kitten or puppy, they may get used to it.

8 AVOID DRY, FLAKY SKIN

To help prevent a dog's skin becoming dry and flaky, add a tiny amount of vegetable oil to its diet each day – a couple of drops for a small dog and up to 1 tsp for a larger one. Give cats fish oil or sardines every week.

9 GROOM OFTEN

Make a habit of grooming your pet at least once a week. Do this job outdoors, and have the least allergic person in your family do it.

10 AVOID ALLOWING PETS IN THE BEDROOM

Don't allow pets in bedrooms or on beds. Keep them out by shutting the bedroom doors. Wherever possible, you should also keep them off soft furnishings.

Room-freshening kit

Fresh air gets rid of most smells, so your first line of attack should be to air your home as often as possible. Also use an extractor fan or open the window while you cook, and shut the kitchen door so smells don't permeate everywhere. Before you turn to chemical air-freshening products, try a natural remedy. For instance, you can remove kitchen smells by simmering a pan of water with cloves and orange peel.

SPRAY BOTTLE
Use to scent the air with a drop or two of your favourite essential oil mixed with water.

SCENTED CANDLES
The more expensive ones are better as the perfumes used are more likely to be natural.

CLOVE-STUDDED ORANGE
Leave this easy-to-make traditional remedy in a bowl to scent a room.

ESSENTIAL OILS
Use your favourites in a water spray or a burner. Good ones to try are lavender, rose, geranium, and orange.

HOUSEPLANTS
Peace lilies
(Spathiphyllum wallisii),
spider plants
(Chlorophytum
comosum), and palms
such as Chamaedorea
elegans are all easy to
grow and do a good job
of absorbing pollutants
in the air.

LAVENDER BAGS
Use for freshening
drawers and cupboards.

Decluttering

10 TIPS Effective decluttering

The aim of decluttering is to get rid of things you don't use and make the most of those you do. To give yourself an incentive to declutter, imagine everything you'll be able to do with the extra space once you've decluttered a cupboard or entire room.

1 HAVE BAGS AND BOXES READY
Arm yourself with bin bags for collecting broken items or things that are obviously rubbish, bags for items you're taking to the charity shop or giving to friends, and storage boxes for the things you end up keeping.

2 LABEL THINGS
When you store things away in boxes, make sure you label them with sticky labels and marker pens. It's easy to think you'll never forget what's inside a box, but the fact is you probably will.

3 CLEAN AS YOU GO
Take the opportunity to give empty drawers and cupboards a quick wipe clean while you're decluttering. You may wish to line clothes drawers with scented paper.

4 BE TOUGH
Try to balance the sentimental value of an object with practical concerns such as how much storage space you have and how useful the item really is.

5 ASK YOURSELF THE MAGIC QUESTIONS
The questions to ask are these: Does the item work? Do you use it? Will you remember where it is? If the answer to any of these is "no", you need to recycle the item, store it elsewhere, or throw it out.

6 RE-GIFT
Unused gifts can make fabulous presents for someone else. Use a sticky note to mark who the gift came from so you avoid giving it back to the person who gave it to you.

7 ONE IN, ONE OUT
For every new item you bring into your home, try to find one that you can recycle or dispose of.

8 BIN AS A LAST RESORT
Only when you've failed to sell an item, give it to a charity shop, recycle it, or reuse it, can you justify sending it to landfill.

9 SET LIMITS
Don't try to reorganize your entire home in one go or you'll end up giving up in defeat. Instead tackle one room at a time and set a time limit for the session.

10 MAKE A MESS
Don't be scared to make things look worse first. It's impossible to do a good job of decluttering without making a mess. Only by making a mess can you then restore order.

10 TIPS Efficient recycling

Landfill sites are filling up fast, so we should avoid adding to them. Luckily, you can recycle almost anything – and sometimes earn money at the same time. So when you're busy decluttering your home, bear in mind the following recycling tips.

1 KEEP A CHARITY BOX
Keep a box at home to store clothes, shoes, and other household items you decide you don't want. Then every so often you can offer things to friends or family, or take them to your local charity shop.

2 MAKE MONEY
There are many ways of turning your unwanted items into cash. Sell them via an online site such as eBay or on sites where postings are free, or make a few pounds by selling them at a car boot sale.

3 GET RID OF LARGE APPLIANCES
If your old fridge, freezer, washing machine, tumble dryer, or microwave is still in good working order, a local charity may accept it to offer to a needy family. Otherwise, see if your council will take it away and recycle it.

4 DONATE FURNITURE
Plenty of charities will collect furniture that you've grown tired of. Alternatively, look out for the Freecycle™ online message board, which enables you to offer furniture and other items you don't want.

5 RECYCLE ELECTRONIC EQUIPMENT
Unwanted mobile phones, MP3 players, and computers can all be recycled. In some cases, computers can be overhauled and sent to developing countries. Check online to find your local recycling centre.

6 DONATE BEDDING AND BLANKETS
Don't throw out old bedding and blankets. Instead, wash them and donate to a homeless shelter or charity shop. Vets and animal shelters also need supplies of towels, sheets, and blankets.

7 RECYCLE CDS AND DVDS
If you can't find a school or charity shop that will have your unwanted CDs and DVDs, look online to find companies that can recycle them and their packaging in an environmentally friendly way.

8 SWAP BOOKS
If you want to offload some books and replace them for free, look out for book-swapping websites. You submit the books you want to get rid of and you get access to an online library to choose your replacements.

9 REDUCE
"Reduce, Reuse, Recycle" is the green mantra. The first step is to reduce. This means buying less in the first place. And when you do buy, choose the best quality you can afford so that it lasts longer.

10 CLOSE THE LOOP
Buying products made from recycled items is just as important as recycling because it creates a demand. Try to buy as many household products and as much clothing made from recycled materials as you can.

Organize audio-visual equipment

Wherever there's audio-visual equipment, there's clutter. To save wasting time looking for a specific item – or worse, falling over it – invest in some storage kit. That way, things will always be to hand.

BARE ESSENTIALS

remote-control tidy

cable organizer

CD and DVD storage unit

gaming station

→1

→2

It's easy to waste time looking for the remote control when you need it. Stow it away in a remote-control tidy to help keep the room uncluttered.

Trailing cables can be hazardous. Either tuck them under the carpet or along the skirting board or, better still, gather them together in a cable organizer.

Extra tips

Declutter your equipment further by using wall-mounting kits where possible.

Declutter your music collection completely by transferring it all to your computer or MP3 player. But always keep a backup on an external hard drive.

Minimise the number of cables you have to plug into the power sockets by using an extension lead that incorporates several sockets. Make sure it's surge-protected to avoid damage to your electrical equipment in the event of a power surge. Some extension leads save energy by automatically switching off all the devices that are plugged in when the main device is switched off.

→3

CDs and DVDs can take up a lot of space. Keep the room uncluttered and the discs dust-free by storing them in their boxes and stacking them in a storage unit.

→4

Keep your games console and games neatly stored in a "gaming station". Get your family into the habit of putting these items away after use.

Pots and pans storage

An efficient kitchen will have everything to hand in the place where you need it. For ease of use, store frequently used pots, pans, and cooking implements near the hob and the oven. Saucepans and their lids take up a lot of room, but fortunately there are a number of storage devices on the market to choose from. Today's modern kitchens often have deep drawers and these can help solve your pan-storage problems.

PAN LID HOLDER
Pan lids are notoriously difficult to store, but use one of these to provide a home for them. If you have enough cupboard space, put the pan-lid holder there.

BAKING EQUIPMENT STORAGE
Deep drawers are a pan-storage boon, especially now that many ovens don't have a storage drawer underneath. Reserve a deep drawer for your baking tins and trays.

STORAGE FOR LESS-USED ITEMS
Keep a low, deep drawer for pots and pans that you use less often.

PAN STANDS
Store bulky pans on a pan stand to free up cupboard space for other, less frequently used items.

HANGING RAIL AND HOOKS
Fix one of these on the wall close to your hob so your cooking implements will be close at hand. S-shaped hooks fit most handles.

Kitchen cupboard storage

Everyone's kitchen cupboards are different. Yours should contain the foods you use regularly, plus one or two items to keep in store in case you can't get to the shops. To save wastage, don't overstock. Check the contents of your cupboard every month and bring items that are nearing their use-by date to the front so you use them in time and don't have to throw them away.

PRESERVING JARS
Use these for storing dry goods or home-made jams and preserves. Store open packages of dried goods in them too. That way you can keep a check on the use-by date.

BOTTLED FOOD
Keep items you use regularly near the front, but check the use-by dates from time to time.

SPICE RACK
Keep only small quantities of herbs and spices as they quickly lose their pungency. A revolving spice rack makes it easy to find the item you're looking for.

CANNED FOOD
This usually has a long shelf life but, as with bottled food, check the use-by dates regularly and bring the oldest items to the front. Never store half-used cans as there's a risk of contamination. Instead, always decant and refrigerate in an airtight, covered container.

CRACKER TIN
Store crackers and crispbreads in a moisture- and dust-proof tin.

TALL CONTAINERS
Use tall glass containers to store spaghetti, fusilli lunghi, and any other long pasta shapes. The container keeps insects, dust, and moisture out, and you can see the contents at a glance.

CEREAL DISPENSER
Decant breakfast cereals into an airtight, moisture-proof dispenser to keep them dry and fresh for longer. A spout means you can pour the contents straight into your cereal bowl.

BISCUIT JAR
Use a wide-bellied biscuit jar to keep biscuits dry. Biscuits quickly absorb moisture from the air if left in an open package.

20 MIN Declutter a kitchen drawer

We all have a junk-filled drawer and it's often in the kitchen. The problem is that we waste precious time trying to find things. Declutter the drawer in minutes and you'll never lose that essential item again.

BARE ESSENTIALS

vacuum cleaner

crevice nozzle

sponge, plastic folders

ziplock bags, old envelopes

labels, drawer organizer

→1

→2

Start by emptying everything out of the drawer. Vacuum inside with the crevice nozzle, then wipe the interior with a damp sponge to pick up any remaining debris.

Arrange the contents of the drawer, putting like with like so it's easy to see what's misplaced and needs to be put back correctly, and what to recycle or throw out

Extra tips

When you return items to the decluttered drawer, put those you use often near the front and those you use less frequently towards the back.

While you're sorting the drawer, ask yourself the magic questions of decluttering (see p.193).

When you return something to a cluttered drawer, take a few minutes to declutter it there and then. If you really can't spare the time straight away, be sure you return to do it within the week.

→3

Store instruction manuals in plastic folders with their receipts. Put flyers and business cards in old envelopes. Stow other items in plastic bags – labelled if necessary.

→4

Replace the items whose home is the kitchen drawer. Don't overfill the drawer or you'll waste time looking for things. Use a drawer organizer if you wish.

Fridge storage

How and where you store food in your fridge, and how long you store it for are all important food-safety factors. Different areas of the fridge cool to slightly different temperatures, which is why it's important to store food in the correct area. Overall, the temperature inside your fridge should be 3°–5°C (37.4°–41°F). Bacteria multiply fast at higher temperatures. If you don't know how cool your fridge is, invest in a thermometer and adjust the temperature if necessary. Finally, always wrap food correctly, and never keep it too long.

DAIRY PRODUCTS
Keep cheese and other dairy products well wrapped on the top shelf. Soft cheeses should keep for a week, hard cheeses for up to 3 weeks.

COOKED MEAT
Keep separate from raw meat. Store for 3–4 days in a glass dish covered with cling film. Check the box to see if the cling film is suitable for contact with the food. If it's not, stretch the film over the dish.

RAW MEAT AND POULTRY
Store for 3–5 days. Keep well wrapped in the lower part of the fridge to avoid blood dripping. The blood may carry bacteria that can contaminate other food. Once meat is cooked, the risk of contamination falls.

FRESH VEGETABLES
Store these on the lower shelves for up to a week, depending on the type of vegetable. To avoid waste, check what you've got daily and use in soups and stir-fries before they wilt.

FRESH FRUIT
Some fruit will keep for 2 weeks in the fridge but, as with fresh vegetables, check regularly and use as quickly as possible.

MILK
Store milk in the fridge door to keep it within easy reach. It will keep from 1 to 2 weeks, depending on the fat content. Keep the container closed.

LEFTOVERS
Store leftovers in airtight lidded containers so they don't dry out. Try and eat within 2–4 days.

FRIDGE DOOR
The temperature of the shelves in the door fluctuates more than in the main cabinet, so don't store highly perishable foods, such as fresh meat or fish, there. Don't open the door more than necessary and always close it as soon as possible.

LEMON FRESHENER
Sprinkle half a lemon with bicarbonate of soda to keep the fridge smelling fresh. Replace as necessary, but at least every 2 weeks.

FRUIT DRINKS
Store these in the door or in the main compartment. Unopened cartons of fresh – non-heat-treated – juice will last up to 3 weeks, but you should use the contents of opened cartons in 7–10 days.

Freezer storage

Freezers are great for long-term food storage, but the bigger your freezer, the more chance you've got of leaving food in it for too long. Yes, even frozen food can spoil! Check the contents of your freezer every few weeks so you don't forget to use what's in it or, better still, keep a magnetic notebook fixed on the door with a list of what you put inside and when. Wrap food carefully to exclude as much air as possible and to keep food in peak condition, and if you're home-freezing, label everything with the date of freezing. But most important of all, you must keep your freezer at -18°C (-4°F) or below.

ICE PACKS
Have these accessible at the top of the freezer and use them for keeping picnic food cool or for keeping food cool while you clean the fridge.

UNFROZEN FOOD
When adding unfrozen items to the freezer, sandwich them between frozen ones so they freeze more quickly.

HOME-MADE MEALS
Store these in freezer-to-oven containers covered with aluminium foil, then you can take them out of the freezer and put them straight in the oven. Store for 4–6 months.

FISH PRODUCTS
Check recommended storage times on the packaging. Fresh fish storage times range from 4 months for oily fish to 10 months for flat fish.

UNCOOKED MEAT
Store on the bottom shelf to avoid it dripping on other items. Fresh meat can be stored for up to a year, depending on the type and cut.

ICE LOLLIES
Keep these on a shallow shelf, then they'll be easier to find.

ICE CUBES
Store on the top shelf so food doesn't leak onto them.

ICE CREAM
Keep this accessible and near the top. Bought ice cream should keep for 6 months.

FROZEN FRUIT AND VEGETABLES
If home-frozen, keep in labelled freezer bags fastened with clips or wire ties and marked with the date of freezing. Home-frozen fruit keeps for 8 months to a year and home-frozen vegetables for up to a year. Commercially frozen fruit keeps for a year and vegetables for 12–18 months.

BREAD PRODUCTS
Store these all together for up to 3 months.

LEFTOVER FOOD
Store this, together with home-made soups and fruit purées, in freezer-proof lidded containers. Label with the date and contents. Store food that includes cooked meat or poultry for 2–6 months.

INDIVIDUAL PORTIONS
Divide items such as sausages into single portions and store in sealed, labelled plastic bags. It's hard to separate individual items when they're frozen together. Store bacon and sausages for 1–2 months.

FROZEN POULTRY
Store chicken or turkey for a maximum of a year.

10 TIPS Decluttering the hall

All too often, the hallway becomes a dumping ground for things you're in too much of a rush to sort out when you arrive home. Prevent hallway chaos and keep your hall organized and clutter-free by following these easy tips.

1 STORE IN A CUPBOARD
Your first line of attack for a clutter-free hall is providing somewhere to stow coats, jackets, hats, scarves, and bags. A hall cupboard is the tidiest solution. Failing that, use wall-mounted hooks.
✓

2 BE TIDY
Encourage the family to hang up their outdoor clothes as soon as they come into the house, unless the clothes are wet, in which case, see tip 3. And encourage them not to dump things in the hall as they pass.
✓

3 DRY OFF WET CLOTHES
Never put damp clothes away in a cupboard or they'll get musty and mildewed. Attach a discreet over-door hook to the hall cupboard door or to another door and hang wet outdoor clothing there.
✓

4 KEEP UP WITH THE SEASONS
Don't waste precious space by keeping out-of-season outdoor clothing in the hall. Instead, sort through what you've got every spring and autumn, and store the things you don't need (see pp.210 and 213).
✓

5 BE SELECTIVE

Don't use the hallway as the place to store all the family's accessories. Select the bags, scarves, and hats you use regularly and put the rest in drawers and cupboards elsewhere in the home.

6 USE A SHOE RACK

If you have a "shoes-off" rule in your house, stand a shoe rack in the hallway to keep shoes neat and tidy. You may be able to fit a shoe rack in the hall cupboard if you have one, which will be even tidier.

7 PICK UP THE MAIL

If mail is delivered through your letter box and lands on the hall floor, don't leave it there to add to the clutter. Pick it up straight away and put letters in a tray to deal with later. Recycle junk mail and unwanted flyers.

8 STORE KEYS SAFELY

Don't leave keys on a hall table or hanging from a peg in the hallway. A burglar might be able to access them through the letter box. Instead fix key hooks or a secure key box on the kitchen wall.

9 CLEAR THE RUBBISH

Don't keep rubbish bags in the hallway waiting to be taken outside. They smell, may leak on the floor, and add to the clutter. Instead, take them from the kitchen to the dustbin as soon as they are full.

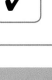

10 USE A BASKET

Have a basket at the bottom of the stairs to collect things that have to be taken up. This keeps the hallway clutter-free, but make sure you keep the basket somewhere you won't fall over it.

20 MIN Declutter a wardrobe

At least once a year, sort through the contents of your wardrobe. It only takes a few minutes and you'll be left with a beautifully decluttered wardrobe where you can find just what you need in a moment.

BARE ESSENTIALS

under-bed storage boxes and/or moisture- and dust-proof clothes storage bags

selection of clothes hangers

→1

Arrange the contents of your wardrobe in piles. One pile is to give to the charity shop, one is for washing or dry-cleaning, and one is for keeping.

→2

Now sort through the pile of clothes you are keeping. Pack unseasonal clothes away in under-bed storage boxes or in moisture- and dust-proof storage bags.

Extra tips

Be ruthless. If you haven't worn something for over two years, it's time to give it to a friend or pass it on to the charity shop.

Don't hang heavy knitwear or long knitted dresses on hangers or they'll lose their shape. Instead, fold them and store them in a drawer or on a shelf.

As you declutter your clothing, check for moth damage. If there is any and it's not too bad, have the clothing dry-cleaned. This will kill any moths and larvae. Throw out damaged clothing and, to prevent future problems, use moth repellant (see p.213) and keep checking the wardrobe every few weeks.

→3

Place clothes on hangers. Don't ruin the shape of clothes by using wire hangers. Use wooden, plastic, or padded hangers, and clip hangers for trousers and skirts.

→4

As you replace items in the wardrobe, keep like with like to help you find items quickly. Group jackets, trousers, suits, skirts, dresses, blouses, and shirts.

Caring for clothes and shoes

The secret to keeping clothes in tip-top condition is having clean, well-organized storage space and never putting dirty clothes away. Moths are your number one enemy, but follow these simple tips, and your clothes will last for years.

1 CLEAN OUT DRAWERS AND WARDROBES
A couple of times a year, empty all drawers and wardrobes, vacuum thoroughly, wash, rinse, and leave to dry. Line shelves and drawers with lining paper. This all helps to deter moths.

✓

2 KEEP MOTHS AT BAY
Check clothing twice a year for signs of moth damage. Either dispose of damaged clothing or have it dry-cleaned to kill the larvae. Deter moths with lavender sachets and cedarwood blocks in drawers and cupboards.

✓

3 ALTERNATE YOUR CLOTHING
Avoid wearing the same clothes or shoes on two consecutive days. Clothes last longer and look fresher if they have a chance to air. Hang clothes up while still warm from the body and the creases will drop out.

✓

4 KEEP CLOTHES IN SHAPE
When hanging up clothes, fasten the top, middle, and bottom buttons, do up the zips and empty all the pockets. Don't over-fill your wardrobe – clothes need space or they'll get musty – and don't hang heavy knitwear.

✓

5 AVOID UNNECESSARY WASHING

Washing clothes too often can lead to them fading and fraying.
If you've only worn an item briefly and it's not dirty, hang it to air
overnight in a well-ventilated place before putting it away.

6 STORE UNSEASONAL CLOTHES

Sort through your clothes every spring and autumn. Wash or dry-clean
unseasonal clothing – moths like dirty clothes – repair if necessary,
then store in dustproof bags, boxes, suitcases, or trunks.

7 GROUP UNDERWEAR

Use separate drawers for bras, pants, knickers, and socks, or use a
drawer organiser to create separate compartments in one drawer.
Store bras with one cup inside the other so they keep their shape.

8 KEEP SHOES IN PAIRS

Store shoes in pairs on a shoe rack, in a canvas hanging organiser, or
in labelled boxes or boxes with a clear window so you can see which
pair is inside.

9 DRY WET SHOES THOROUGHLY

If shoes are very wet, pack them with newspaper or kitchen towel and
leave them to dry naturally before putting them away. This will stop
them going out of shape.

10 STOP SHOES SMELLING

Sprinkle the inside of smelly shoes with bicarbonate of soda and leave
them overnight. Next morning, shake or vacuum the powder out.

Home office storage

You'll work more efficiently in your home office when everything you need is tidy and close at hand. Gather up all your clutter by using storage trays, desk tidies, and filing systems, but choose items that suit your specific needs, or you'll simply end up with a clutter of storage solutions. And no matter how long you spend at your desk, invest in a good chair. It's better for your back – and when your back's comfortable, your mind will be clearer.

DESK CHAIR
Make sure your desk chair is comfortable. At a minimum it should provide good lumbar – low-back – support, must be height-adjustable, and have lockable castors. Ideally, it should also support the sacrum – the bone at the base of the spine – and the depth of the seat and the arms should all be adjustable.

FILING TRAYS
Stackable trays save space on your desk. Use to hold papers that you need as you work, as well as papers that are waiting to be filed away.

DESK TIDY
Choose one with a number of different-sized compartments to hold pens, pencils, paperclips, rubber bands, and all the other small office paraphernalia you need.

HOME FILE
Buy one that contains hanging files and use it for storing papers that you only need occasionally. If you're short of shelf space, keep it on the floor, but not where you might fall over it.

DOCUMENT WALLETS
Use these to keep papers together for the projects that you're currently working on.

STICKY NOTES
Have a variety of sizes and colours for different purposes.

MAGAZINE FILE
Store magazines and brochures here and, if you're short of space, sort them regularly and throw away any you no longer need.

WASTE BASKET
Essential for helping to keep your home office tidy. If you have room, you could have two baskets – one for recyclable material.

Declutter an attic or basement

10 TIPS

An attic or basement may seem to offer the ultimate storage solution, but if you don't plan your storage properly, these rooms can soon lapse into chaos. Follow these simple, methodical tips for clutter-free storage that works.

1 DO A CULL
Before you begin, take a long, hard look at what you've got. Do you really need it? Have you used it in the last year? Have you missed it? If any of your answers are "no", then donate the item, sell it, or throw it out.

2 START TO SEPARATE
Now assess what you've got left to store, and everything else will follow. Separate what's seasonal from what needs short- or long-term storage, then plan what containers you'll need and in which sizes.

3 ACCESS AND LIGHT
Review your storage space and plan to put the things you need to access most often nearest the door. Make sure, too, that the room's well lit so when you do need something, you don't have to grope in the dark.

4 GET THE RIGHT STORAGE
Choose storage that does the job. Make sure it fits the things you're keeping and that it's dust- and damp-proof. Stackable storage will help to save space.

5 LABEL, LABEL, LABEL

The only way to find things quickly is to label them, and in general, the bigger the labels, the better. What's more, when a thing's labelled, you can send someone else to find it.

6 USE THE WALLS

Make the most of the wall space by putting up hooks and attaching plenty of shelving. This not only helps keep the floor clear, but gives you somewhere to store smaller items.

7 KEEP A PATH CLEAR

There's no point storing stuff if you can't get to it. Make sure you leave a clear path through the boxes and don't fill the entire floor space.

8 LEAVE SPACE IN CONTAINERS

Chances are there are stairs to your attic or basement, in which case, don't overfill your storage containers and make them too heavy. When you need to get them out, you don't want to risk injury.

9 KEEP A NOTE

Keep a note of everything you've stored away and where exactly you've put it. Months and occasionally years might pass before you need a particular item and it may be very hard to remember where it is.

10 KEEP IT CLEAN

There's nothing worse than having to deal with dusty, cobwebby boxes. Once a year, take everything out of storage, dust the containers, and vacuum or sweep the floor.

10 TIPS Running a thrifty household

It's wise not to waste your money – or the earth's resources. These thrifty tips cover everything from budgeting to food and from cleaning to clothes care. Follow these pain-free suggestions and you'll be well on the way to running a truly thrifty household.

1 SAVE ENERGY
Turn lights off when you leave a room, keep thermostats low and wear an extra layer, reduce your water usage, buy energy-efficient electrical goods – all these will save you money as well as save the planet.

2 HAVE A BUDGET
There are good budget planners online that will show you how much you spend each year and what you spend it on. If you're spending more than you earn, the planner will help you see where to cut back.

3 BE A CLEVER SHOPPER
Always arm yourself with a shopping list, don't shop for food when you're hungry, and only shop once a week. These are tried-and-tested tips that will save you from temptation.

4 BUY CHEAP
When you're shopping for everyday items, buy the cheapest product that does the job effectively. Save by buying in bulk and if you can bear it, cut out meat and see your food bills plummet.

5 KEEP THE FREEZER FULL

A full freezer uses less electricity than a half-full one, so save money by keeping your freezer as packed as possible. If there are large gaps, fill them with old milk cartons filled with water.

6 GROW YOUR OWN

There's a burgeoning interest in growing your own food. Have a go, even if it's just a few herbs by the kitchen door, some windowsill salads, or a mini fruit tree or tomatoes in a pot.

7 LEARN TO SEW

All you need to know is the basics. Learn how to sew on a button or stitch up a hem. You'll prolong the life of your clothes and save money that you'd otherwise spend on repairs.

8 USE UP PRODUCTS COMPLETELY

To use the last drop of a cleaning product, add a splash of water to the bottle, and to reach the last squeeze of creams and pastes, cut the containers open to reveal what's left inside.

9 GIVE NEW LIFE TO OLD

Use old toothbrushes for scrubbing in hard-to-reach corners and for cleaning grouting, cut up old t-shirts to use as dusters, and use old ice-cream tubs and other lidded food containers for food storage.

10 USE THIS BOOK

The tips in this book will save you money. Keep your home and clothing clean and things will last longer and need replacing less often. Use store-cupboard cleaning products and save money on your weekly shop.

Index

Acknowledgments

Dorling Kindersley would like to thank Tamsin Weston for props styling, Gary Kemp for retouching, Adam Brackenbury for symbols artwork, Tessa Bindloss for design assistance, Danaya Bunnag for modelling and general assistance, Roxanne Benson-Mackey for modelling, Emma Sergeant, Ria Osborne, and Liz Franks for assisting the photographer and for modelling, Hers Agency Ltd. for providing the props stylist, j me for supplying props, and 1st Option for the location house.